The New York Times

CROSSWORDS FOR YOUR BEACH BAG
75 Easy, Breezy Puzzles

Edited by
Will Shortz

ST. MARTIN'S GRIFFIN ※ NEW YORK

ISBN 0-312-31455-8

10 9 8 7 6 5 4

by Gregory E. Paul

1

ACROSS

1 Opera house box
5 Geography book
10 Golfer's alert
14 Gung-ho
15 Aplomb
16 Missing from the Marines, say
17 Trio in Bethlehem
18 Kindergarten adhesive
19 Onionlike plant
20 Noël Coward play
23 Dobbin's nibble
24 Postsurgical program
28 "Total ___" (1990 film)
32 Set free
35 Internet messages
36 "You'd ___ Nice to Come Home To"
37 Trouble
38 "Ho, ho, ho" sayer
42 Ike's W.W. II command
43 Flunky
44 Disney mermaid
45 Arts and crafts class
48 Garb
49 Secret rendezvous
50 Sold-out sign
51 Nickname for Hubert Humphrey, with "the"
59 On ___ (without commitment)
62 Knight's wear
63 Not working
64 Prefix with bucks
65 Drink served with marshmallows
66 Grain for farm animals
67 Atop
68 Get used (to)
69 Town NNE of Santa Fe

DOWN

1 Gentle one
2 Skating rink, e.g.
3 Lerner and Loewe musical
4 Rewrite
5 Sex ___
6 Wedding offering to the bride and groom
7 Daffy Duck's impediment
8 Italian wine region
9 Psychic
10 Stumble
11 Be in arrears
12 Future flounder
13 Big game animal
21 Christmas decoration
22 Indignation
25 Michener novel
26 Penitent
27 Ladybug, e.g.
28 Veto
29 Ham
30 Dieter's unit: Var.
31 Be bedridden
32 Yorkshire city
33 "Uh-huh"
34 Rock's ___ Jovi
36 ___-a-brac
39 Moo goo ___ pan
40 University of Florida student
41 N.Y.C. subway
46 Waste receptacle
47 N.Y.C. subway overseer
48 Genesis mountain
50 Hawk's descent
52 White-spotted rodent
53 Egg on
54 Community org. with a gym
55 Break in friendly relations
56 Notion
57 Parkay product
58 Cincinnati nine
59 Home of the Mustangs, for short
60 Oomph
61 It may need massaging

2

by Randall J. Hartman

ACROSS
1 Literary lioness
5 Open a crack
9 Seeing red
14 Painter of limp watches
15 Rational
16 Elicit
17 Road, for Romulus
18 Signs
19 "Drove my Chevy to the ___ . . ." (1972 lyric)
20 1991 feminist movie
23 Old photo
24 Skin layer
25 Radical 60's org.
28 For the taking
30 Give a licking
31 4:00, in Kent
32 300-pound President
35 Dog's drink, or resting spot
37 Bikini alternative
39 Cousin of the English horn
40 Work, as dough
43 Approximately
44 Valerie Harper series
46 "Much ___ About Nothing"
47 Certain grains
48 It thickens the plot
49 Snowball in "Animal Farm"
52 Rounds, say
54 Mythical monster
55 Eye opener
57 Balance sheet plus
61 Cartoon magpies
64 Reluctant
66 Zeno's home
67 Takes care of the squeaky wheel
68 Come together
69 Armed Forces option
70 Sunburn woe
71 It's all in the family
72 Fires
73 Ferber of "Show Boat"

DOWN
1 Blue-pencils
2 Shop tool
3 Result of counting sheep
4 Delivered by a Huey Cobra
5 Home of 3.5 billion
6 "Surf City" singers, 1963
7 It's just over a foot
8 Martha's Vineyard, in the summer
9 Trustful
10 Singer Burl
11 41-week best seller, 1970–71
12 Barely manage, with "out"
13 Gidget portrayer Sandra
21 Deface
22 Actress Thurman
26 Thickheaded
27 Powdered starches
29 Lodge member
32 Common sculpture
33 Hate
34 Ecological succession
36 Princess tormentor
38 Some check it daily
41 Early outcasts
42 Suffix with star or tsar
45 Side in many a western
50 Type
51 Lead ore
53 Screen siren West
56 "Chill!"
58 Went down a slope
59 "Sea of Love" star Barkin
60 Physicist Nikola
62 "___, Brute!"
63 Noisy birds
64 Blockhead
65 Early afternoon

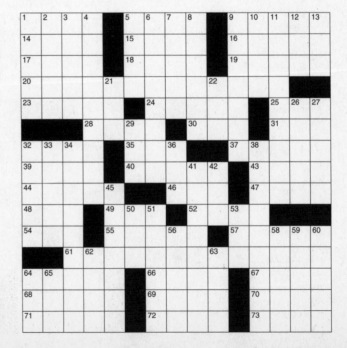

ACROSS

1 Put one's foot down
6 Not stiff
10 Without: Fr.
14 Prefix with anthropology
15 Eye part
16 "Here comes trouble!"
17 Arctic or Indian, e.g.
18 Flees
19 Noose material
20 "Yes!"
22 Ogled
23 Name for many a theater
24 Totally absorbed (in)
26 Bright and bouncy
29 "Get ___ of yourself!"
33 Easter bloom
37 Managed
38 Often-welcomed part of the week
39 Suffix with switch
40 Bara of the silents
42 Lymph ___
43 Interstellar cloud
45 Diamond ___
46 Alum
47 Southwestern home material
48 "___ of Two Cities"
50 Atlantic Seaboard, with "the"
52 Egyptian's tongue
57 Quick
60 "Yes!"
63 Prez
64 So long, in Soho
65 Utter fear
66 Engineer's school
67 Western Indians
68 Court TV coverage
69 Nick and Nora's dog
70 Attention-getter
71 Because

DOWN

1 Mar
2 Tasteless
3 Kind of acid
4 Civil War general
5 Pay
6 One of a kind
7 "Terrible" czar
8 Computer capacity
9 Ziti, e.g.
10 "Yes!"
11 Hey there, at sea
12 Nah
13 Outbuilding
21 Mafioso's code of silence
25 Golfer's goal
27 Cheerleader's cry
28 Genuflected
30 Aroma
31 Terhune's "___ Dog"
32 Like Easter eggs
33 Songstress Horne
34 Enraged
35 Gray wolf
36 "Yes!"
38 Bit of finery
41 A day in Spain
44 Lowing herd's place
48 Baseball stat
49 Gives way to rage
51 ___ and took notice
53 Early name in video games
54 African republic
55 Ending with sacro-
56 Rinse or dry, in a dishwasher
57 Goat cheese
58 Gives the heave-ho
59 Splinter group
61 Holy Fr. ladies
62 Malt kiln

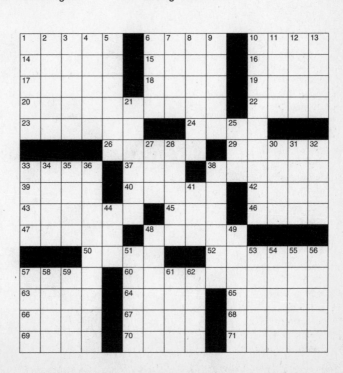

4

by Manny Nosowsky

ACROSS

1 Prelude to a duel
5 Not hearing
9 Competitor for a Clio
14 Seat of Allen County, Kan.
15 Unattractive fruit that sounds that way
16 Upright, e.g.
17 Taking radical action
20 Kiss mark
21 Lamb's kin
22 Wonderment
23 "Bye!"
24 Much too bright
27 Romulus's brother
29 Rundown in appearance
33 Words of woe
37 "Buddy"
38 "23 ___": Var.
39 Holing up
42 Expired
43 Princess of operetta
44 "___ boy!"
45 One who can't go home
46 Give quarters to
48 Laotians, e.g.
50 Mowed strip
55 Breakfast staple
58 Have some tea
59 Sound investment?
60 Civil War story
64 Disconcert
65 Theater award
66 Peak in the "Odyssey"
67 "Same here!"
68 Fishing area
69 Lack

DOWN

1 Lovers' sounds
2 Sarge's boss
3 Restaurant owner of song
4 Hanky-___
5 Scout's pledge word
6 I, to Claudius
7 Inn drink
8 Repairmen
9 Like some mountain lodge activities
10 Conk out
11 Nursery call
12 Freshly
13 It smells a lot
18 Equipment
19 Prefix with light
24 Dillinger fighter
25 Setting for this puzzle's theme
26 Alpine heroine
28 Give off, as light
30 Redo, as text
31 Puts on
32 Eastern discipline
33 Grimm character
34 Martian invasion report, e.g.
35 60's dress style
36 ___ Gay (W.W. II plane)
38 Mass of hair
40 Caller's playful request
41 3:1, 5:2, etc.
46 Portable computer
47 Renaissance name of fame
49 Certain grandson
51 Champions' cry
52 Get up
53 Edgy
54 Nonsurfer at the beach
55 "Omigosh!"
56 Mongolian desert
57 Flying pest
59 Tool repository
61 N.C. and S.C. zone
62 Cable channel
63 Type of type

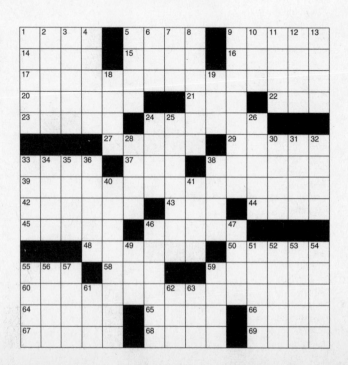

ACROSS

1 Has speech difficulties
6 On ___ (like much freelance work)
10 Opera star
14 Brilliant success
15 Bathroom flooring
16 Japanese sashes
17 Diner offering
20 Hire
21 Partygoer
22 Shakespearean king
24 Historic periods
25 Walter Cronkite's network
28 Plant part
30 Amount eaten
34 The triple of a triple play
36 Org. overseeing fairness in hiring
38 Specified
39 Restaurant offering
42 Week or rear follower
43 Min. components
44 Author ___ Stanley Gardner
45 Emblems on Indian poles
47 Bucks' mates
49 Initials in fashion
50 In ___ land (dreaming)
52 "Three men in ___"
54 Living
58 Apache souvenirs
62 Lawn party offering
64 Sale caveat
65 Swallow
66 Emulate Cicero
67 Used E-mail
68 Verbally joust (with)
69 Continue a subscription

DOWN

1 ___-majesté
2 Computer signpost
3 False coin
4 Like John Paul II
5 Old Wells Fargo vehicles
6 Regular: Abbr.
7 Tower locale
8 Exhilarate
9 Prefix with -fugal
10 Like New York City, to Albany
11 Footnote abbr.
12 Bad habit, so to speak
13 Arthur ___ Stadium (U.S.T.A. facility)
18 Tidy up
19 Actress/singer Durbin
23 Marsh plants
25 Kitchen cleanser
26 It's good in Guadalajara
27 German city
29 Bike that zips in and out of traffic
31 Writer Cleveland ___
32 Starting points in shipbuilding
33 1950's Ford flop
35 Hardest and strongest
37 Drink with a marshmallow
40 Spanish fleet
41 Pesky African insect
46 Broken arm holders
48 Aid and comfort
51 Ending words in a price
53 Wilkes-___, Pa.
54 They were once "The most trusted name in television"
55 Facility
56 Injure, as a knee
57 ___ monster
59 Not having much fat
60 Cracker topping
61 Eurasian duck
63 Life-saving skill, for short

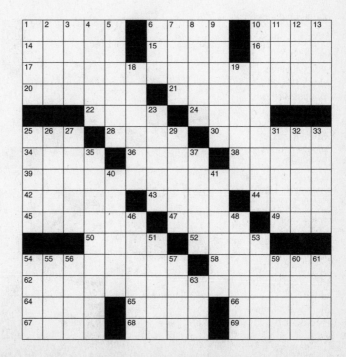

6 by William S. Cotter

ACROSS

1 Bay of Naples isle
6 Custard base
9 Hamburger, e.g.
14 Marriage
15 Word for a superior
16 Nebraska's biggest city
17 Pipe parts
18 Sports Illustrated's 1974 Sportsman of the Year
19 Not so strict
20 "Impossible" achievement
23 Poly-___ (college major)
24 Faux pas
25 Language name suffix
28 Excise
30 Strikingly unusual things
35 March Madness org.
37 Offshore apparatus
39 Prohibitions for Junior
40 "Impossible" discovery
44 Reach in amount
45 Parisian article
46 Toy on a string
47 Not always
50 Furry TV alien
52 Beachgoer's goal
53 Andy's boy, in 60's TV
55 One of ___ own
57 "Impossible" activity!
65 Angler of morays
66 Holm of "Chariots of Fire"
67 More than some
68 Kind of acid
69 English ___

70 Goosebump-raising
71 Inner connection?
72 "Don't Bring Me Down" rock grp.
73 Not neatniks

DOWN

1 Zodiacal delineation
2 Get the pot going
3 Dock
4 Frolics
5 Bug
6 Birthright seller, in Genesis
7 Poisonous desert dwellers, for short
8 Radiator front
9 Sportsman's mount
10 Amo, amas, ___

11 Curbside call
12 Lt. Kojak
13 Kitten's plaything
21 Pageant topper
22 Variety
25 Prefix with structure
26 Reconnoiterer
27 Visit again and again
29 Top of a clock dial
31 Was in, as a class
32 Eskimo
33 Terra ___
34 Visibly frightened
36 Voting "no"
38 African antelope
41 It's another day
42 Out ___ limb
43 One who has life to look forward to?
48 Smog-battling org.

49 Pretty as a picture, e.g.
51 "Killing Me Softly" pop group, with "the"
54 Quick communication
56 "Boléro" composer
57 They may be strained in young families
58 Do-___ (cabbage)
59 Actress Lena
60 Biological trait carrier
61 Enjoying, in slang
62 ___ Beach, Fla.
63 Tot's place
64 Whiskies

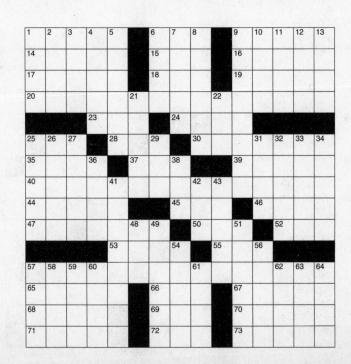

by William Canine

7

ACROSS

1 Essence
5 Fable finale
10 ___ facto
14 London district
15 Fruit container
16 See 47-Across
17 1944 Oscar-winning song by Bing Crosby
20 Jobs to do
21 Radiant
22 Inflation-fighting W.W. II org.
23 Vote of support
24 Actor Gibson
25 Years and years
27 Oats for horses, say
29 Hotel capacity
30 Commence
33 Pie ___ mode
34 Start of a counting-out rhyme
35 Like some Jewish delis
36 Berlin's home: Abbr.
37 Court divider
38 Like 10-watt bulbs
39 Friend in France
40 Not give up an argument
42 Spy's writing
43 Litter member
44 Japanese camera
45 Middle ears?
46 Church niche
47 With 16-Across, depressed
48 Doc bloc
49 Wield
50 Sure-footed work animal
52 Send, as money
54 Send elsewhere
57 1951 hit with music by former Veep Dawes

60 Christmastime
61 Go fishing
62 Tiptop
63 Soviet news agency
64 They're counted at meetings
65 See 45-Down

DOWN

1 "Hey there!"
2 Hawkeye State
3 1937 Benny Goodman hit
4 Reacted like a taxi driver?
5 Sprint rival
6 Embellish
7 Tattered
8 The Marshall Islands, e.g.
9 Jay who has Monday night "Headlines"
10 Conditions
11 1960 song from "Bye Bye Birdie"
12 Polaroid
13 Gumbo plant
18 Fed. property overseer
19 Stunning
26 Extra-play periods, for short
27 Dickens thief
28 1983 Nicholas Gage book
29 Red vegetable
31 Tale-spinning Uncle
32 Rubbish
34 Tangle up
35 Youngsters

38 Fight (with)
41 Charged particle
42 ___ and goings
45 With 65-Across, a Spanish highway
46 Sour brew
49 ___-Raphaelite
50 "It ___ pretty!"
51 Portico
53 Verve
55 Austen heroine
56 Stagger
58 Smith and Gore
59 "For ___ a jolly . . ."

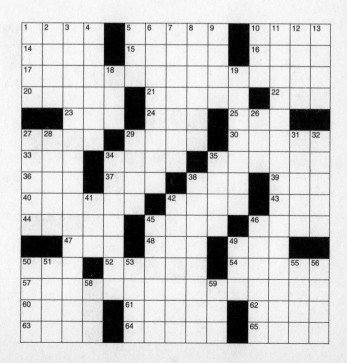

8

by Jonathan Schmalzbach

ACROSS
1. Moby-Dick chaser
5. Hobble
9. Alternative if things don't work out
14. Vincent Lopez's theme song
15. Met highlight
16. Refuges
17. TV turner
18. Bridge, in Bretagne
19. Vowel sound
20. Modern times, to Auden
23. Paris airport
24. Stop ___ dime
25. Nudge, as the memory
28. Copperhead's weapon
30. Snub, in a way
32. One of the Mrs. Sinatras
33. The 1890's, historically
37. Performing ___
39. Acquire
40. Individuals
41. Sherlockian times
46. Scottish refusal
47. Chameleonlike creature
48. Confrere
50. Acquire, slangily
51. Explosive letters
53. Flabbergast
54. The 1980's, to yuppies
59. "East of Eden" director
62. Part of N.B.
63. Christiania, now
64. Brewer Samuel
65. Kind of proportions
66. ___-mutton
67. Sioux dwelling
68. Smaller cousin of 67-Across
69. Expensive

DOWN
1. "Put Your Head on My Shoulder" singer
2. ___ Kong
3. Tissue softener
4. Coarse dimwit
5. One of the Canary Islands
6. Often-missed humor
7. Impudent girl
8. Lanai
9. Stamps
10. Gossamer
11. Cigar leaving
12. Novel
13. Jamboree grp.
21. "Pennies ___ Heaven"
22. Home of Phillips University
25. Actress Barnes or Kerns
26. Severe test
27. Skein formers
28. Ill-tempered woman
29. Devours
31. Cpl., e.g.
32. Like Mann's mountain
34. "That's awful!"
35. Dog doc
36. Summer on the Riviera
38. 70's terrorist org.
42. Like some gazes
43. The Daltons, for example
44. Take back
45. Greenish-blue
49. Countless
52. Ism
53. Take effect
54. Broadway musical with the song "We Need a Little Christmas"
55. "Huh-uh"
56. "Things are becoming clear"
57. Masha and Irina's sister, in Chekhov
58. Queen of Jordan
59. Krazy ___
60. Fruity quaff
61. Last sound some bugs hear

by Evie Eysenburg

ACROSS

1 Total
4 Castle protector
8 Sipper's aid
13 "___ tu" (Verdi aria)
14 Open, as a gate
16 Rapid-fire
17 Beavers' project
18 Former Bangkok-based grp.
19 Yens
20 Question of understanding, to a Spanish count?
23 Undemanding, as a job
24 Recede
25 "___ girl watcher" (1968 song lyric)
28 Actor Morales
29 Plant again
32 Boast
33 "The Old Wives' Tale" dramatist George
35 "Ars Poetica" poet
37 What a doctor prescribes, to a Spanish count?
40 Lacking interest
41 "Same here"
42 Harvest
43 Important element of rap lyrics
45 Where baby sleeps
49 ___ Lanka
50 Coffee alternative
51 Alan Ladd western
52 Minute nutritional components, to a Spanish count?
56 House V.I.P. Dick
59 Cease-fire
60 Cause for a Band-Aid
61 Perjurers
62 Swashbuckling Flynn
63 Word repeated in "takes ___ to know ___"
64 Slight contamination
65 Mailed
66 Bloodshot

DOWN

1 Tempt
2 Planet beyond Saturn
3 Brunch drink
4 Like cooked oatmeal
5 Prime draft classification
6 Blind as ___
7 Jacques of French cinema
8 Edible pigeon
9 Swirl
10 Trucker's truck
11 Serve that zings
12 Divs. of months
15 He was asked "Wherefore art thou?"
21 Creates quickly
22 "Charlotte's Web" author
25 Shah's land, once
26 Anti-attacker spray
27 "___ before beauty"
29 "Foul!" caller
30 Shade provider
31 Rundown
32 Sweet roll
34 Long, long time
36 World Series mo.
37 Stags and does
38 Town east of Santa Barbara
39 Barely lit
40 P.S.A.T. takers
44 Swiftness
46 Ill will
47 What musical instruments should be
48 Defeated
50 Rendezvous
51 Relative of the salmon
52 Graceful aquatic bird
53 Goes astray
54 Tempt
55 Supply-and-demand subj.
56 Not the main route: Abbr.
57 Narrow inlet
58 ___ tai

10

by Elizabeth C. Gorski

ACROSS

1 Won't-keep-you-up-at-night beverage
6 Improvisation
11 Hon
14 Beethoven dedicatee
15 The supreme Supreme
16 Simile's center
17 Not discreet
19 Rendezvoused
20 Mekong River land
21 English university city
23 Fixes securely
27 Morsel
29 Whole
30 Kind of microscope
33 Plucked instruments
34 Put (down), as money
35 Power serve, perhaps
36 London "stops"
37 Rounded the edges of
38 Catcher's catcher
39 Advice giver Landers
40 Fragrant trees
41 French legislature
42 Portions
44 Word before Highness
45 Not in port
46 Broke off (from)
47 Poem
49 Portion
50 Video maker, for short
51 Hardly generous
58 Numbered rd.
59 Up ___ (stuck)
60 Maine university town
61 Frowning
62 Puts in an overhead compartment, say
63 Three trios

DOWN

1 Dover's state: Abbr.
2 "Do Ya" group, for short
3 A.F.L.-___
4 Dummkopf
5 They're put out at times
6 "See ya!"
7 Ballroom dance maneuvers
8 Napkin's place
9 Like Bach's Violin Sonata No. 3
10 Casino affliction
11 Not too smart
12 Preowned
13 Chocolate factory sights
18 Highway division
22 C.P.R. expert
23 "You guys . . ."
24 "Tennis, ___?"
25 Bullied
26 Father's Day favorites
27 This puzzle has 78
28 Tear apart
30 Some fashion magazines
31 Gas rating
32 Snared
34 One of Columbus's ships
37 Rare-coin rating
38 French mother
40 Madrid money
41 Arrondissement, in Paris
43 Holyoke and Sinai, e.g.: Abbr.
44 Slave
46 Fills up
47 Some RCA products
48 "I could ___ horse!"
49 Piano mover's cry
52 Blue chip giant
53 Miracle-___ (garden brand)
54 Sold-out inits.
55 Heavy weight
56 Atlanta-to-Raleigh dir.
57 Part of an E-mail address

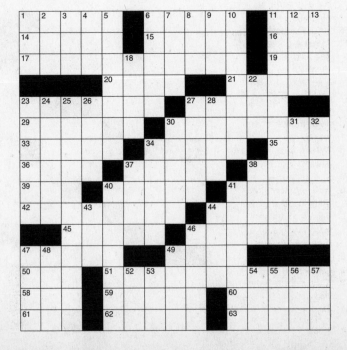

ACROSS

1 Feudal workers
6 Italian money
10 Con artist's art
14 Characteristic
15 Scent
16 Barbershop emblem
17 Indy 500 competitor
18 Suckling spot
19 Landed (on)
20 First step for a would-be groom vis-à-vis his intended's father
23 Director Craven
24 Mauna ___
25 Arrow's path
26 New Deal org.
29 Kind of talk the would-be bride had with mom
32 Commedia dell'___
35 A.F.L.'s partner
36 ___ into holy matrimony
37 Sets of pews
38 Namely
41 "___ pin and pick it up . . ."
42 Bullwinkle, e.g.
44 Opposite of WSW
45 Coffee servers
46 How the would-be groom proposed
50 Actor Fernando
51 Wedding ___
52 Letters on a Cardinal's cap
53 Shoot the breeze
56 What the bride's father did vis-à-vis the reception
60 "Neato!"
62 Director Kazan
63 Kind of lily
64 Dull sound
65 Notes after do
66 Ebb and neap, e.g.
67 Peeved
68 British gun
69 What italics do

DOWN

1 Scarecrow stuffing
2 Wipe out
3 Pool ball sorters
4 Where 1-Across slaved
5 Golf shot
6 Ladies' man
7 ___ fixe
8 Greet with loud laughter
9 Prefix with -pod or -scope
10 Bridge unit
11 It's thrown on bad ideas
12 He K.O.'d Foreman 10/30/74
13 Bumped into
21 Take countermeasures
22 Be in pain
27 Groom carefully
28 Gillette razors
29 "Siddhartha" writer
30 Hauled
31 Follow as a result
32 Knight's garb
33 TV news exec Arledge
34 Common board size
39 Tough job for a dry cleaner
40 Tithe amount
43 Within: Prefix
47 Library gadgets
48 Shoelace hole
49 Votes into office
53 Funny lady Radner
54 Funny man Woody
55 Great time, or great noise
57 Kind of shoppe
58 Onetime phone call cost
59 Get-out-of-jail money
60 Pennies: Abbr.
61 "Well, what's this?!"

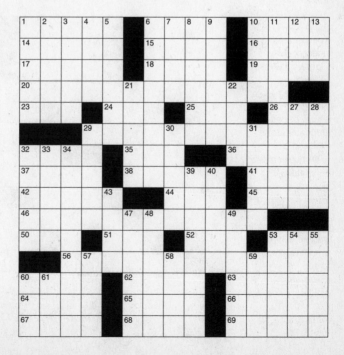

12
by Arthur S. Verdesca

ACROSS
1 Chair part
5 Stuff
9 Blackmore heroine Lorna
14 Salon focus
15 Capital of Latvia
16 Writer Sinclair
17 Meat inspection inits.
18 Journey for Caesar
19 5 to 1, say
20 Best Picture of 1987
23 Der ___ (Adenauer)
24 Malt kiln
25 Neighbor of Chile: Abbr.
28 Woodlands
30 Actress Novak
33 "Vive ___!" (old French cry)
35 Truman's nuclear agcy.
36 Grandma, affectionately
37 Opera by Glinka
41 Others
42 Furrow
43 Nutso
44 Encountered
45 Educator Mary McLeod ___
48 Fifth quarters, so to speak: Abbr.
49 Rip
50 Pres. Reagan and others
52 Popular dish often served with rice
58 Shoot at, as tin cans
59 Excellent
60 Getting ___ years
61 Mooch
62 The "brains" of 58-Down

63 "___ girl!"
64 Saccharine
65 Pianist Myra
66 Missing

DOWN
1 Closed
2 Eye swatter?
3 White House staffer
4 Cheery song syllables
5 "The Count of Monte ___"
6 Singing cowboy Tex
7 Pulitzer writer James
8 Squirrellike monkey
9 Compulsion by force

10 Some 60's paintings
11 Germany's ___ von Bismarck
12 Roulette bet
13 Rock's Brian
21 1966 movie or song hit
22 Quilt part
25 Car protector
26 U.S. Grant opponent
27 Mill fodder
29 Astronauts' returning point
30 Musical toy
31 Unfitting
32 "The Bells of St. ___"
34 Frequently
36 Sgt., e.g.
38 Carnival oddity

39 Community service program
40 "Maria ___" (1941 hit song)
45 St. Thomas who was murdered in a cathedral
46 Seventh planet
47 Surprisingly
49 Slight color
51 Toast
52 Lobster pincer
53 Cover up
54 Slangy denial
55 Engrossed by
56 Pesky insects
57 Pesky insect
58 Modern office staples, for short

ACROSS

1 Sound astonished
5 "Hound Dog" man
10 Chicken bite
14 "Tell ___ My Heart" (1987 hit)
15 Nickels and dimes
16 Author Hunter
17 One who runs a jail?
19 Fiddler while Rome burned
20 Alpha's opposite
21 ___ school (doctor's training)
22 Chronic nag
23 Twisty curve
24 Broach, as a subject
27 Toe woe
28 Direct path
32 Gas pump rating
35 Adds to the mixture
36 Undecided
37 Something to believe
39 "___ kleine Nachtmusik"
40 Overfrequently
42 TV's Greene and Michaels
44 Seasoned vets
45 Pianist Myra
46 First in time
48 Long time
51 Hardly any
54 Chicken ___ king
55 Waned
57 Walk the waiting room
58 Sautéing, jail-style?
60 Partner of "done with"
61 Poke fun at
62 Singer Adams
63 Kennedy and Turner
64 Viper
65 Views

DOWN

1 Army figure
2 Parts of molecules
3 Hogs' homes
4 Ping-___
5 Environmentalist's prefix
6 One at the bottom of the totem pole
7 Grew like ivy
8 Worse than awful, foodwise
9 Kazakhstan, once: Abbr.
10 Jail cells?
11 Always
12 Give a hoot
13 Have memorized
18 Hawk's grabber
22 British submachine gun
25 ___ Set (kid's builder)
26 Pokes fun at
27 Jail keys?
29 "The doctor ___"
30 Prime time hour
31 Chemical endings
32 Director Preminger
33 Groovy
34 Tramped (on)
35 London's Big ___
38 Put back on the agenda
41 "Animal House" grp.
43 Blender maker
45 Final transport
47 Story of Achilles
48 Put up with
49 Magical wish granter
50 Noses (out)
51 TV commercial
52 Bat's home
53 Scored 100 on
56 Tournament passes
58 Train terminal: Abbr.
59 Not agin

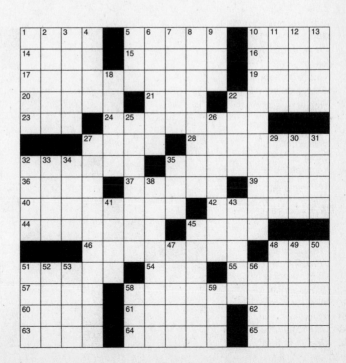

14

by Bill Ballard

ACROSS

1 Carpenter's gadget
6 XXXI times V
9 Hardly spine-tingling
13 Express again
14 China's Chou En-___
15 Capital NW of Twin Falls
16 With 58-Across, a classic line associated with 47-Across
19 Ethel Waters' "___ Blue?"
20 Concert equipment
21 Apprehensively
22 Oscar-winning actor in 47-Across
26 Hope is here: Abbr.
27 Automne preceder
28 "Indubitably"
31 Coeur d'___, Idaho
34 "Your Erroneous Zones" author Wayne
35 I.B.M., e.g.
36 Kind of wagon
38 Section of Queens, N.Y.
40 Yard tool
41 Like ___ out of hell
43 Church cries
44 Wks. and wks.
45 Baby blossom
46 "We ___ the World"
47 Oscar-winning film
53 Inflationary path
56 Inlet
57 Lyric poem
58 See 16-Across
62 Seal fur trader

63 Boeing 737, e.g.
64 Window parts
65 Pioneer's heading
66 Hit show sign
67 Confuse

DOWN

1 "Iliad" king
2 Auxiliary proposition
3 Name on many planes
4 Steamed
5 "Ciao!"
6 What clematis plants do
7 Slippery one
8 Rome's Appia or Veneto
9 Like some B'way performances

10 Biography
11 On the main
12 München mister
15 Link
17 Bit of yarn
18 Frisco gridders
23 Arm of a knight-in-arms
24 Snack that's bitten or licked
25 Corroded
28 Time long past
29 Leprechauns' land
30 Get-well spots
31 Out of whack
32 Limerick maker
33 Lodge fellows
34 Fix a computer program
35 Doomsday cause, maybe

37 Old phone company sobriquet
39 Skater Lipinski
42 Embellisher
46 Many miles away
47 Rainbow ___
48 ___ monde (society)
49 "Same here"
50 Keep after
51 Eponym for failure
52 Dodger Hall-of-Famer
53 "Pygmalion" writer
54 Soccer superstar
55 Boardwalk refreshments
59 Spinners' spinners?
60 Pollution stds. setter
61 Tattoos, currently

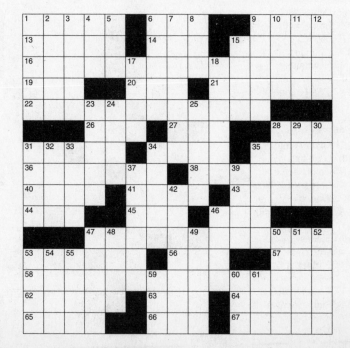

ACROSS

1 Mah-jongg piece
5 "Saved by the ___!"
9 Het up
14 Declare
15 "Garfield" dog
16 Confused struggle
17 Small skirt
18 Chew like a beaver
19 Perfect
20 North Dakota tourist attraction
23 Building annex
24 Attack
25 Campus military org.
27 "Auf wiedersehen" wisher
31 Gymnast Korbut
34 Indian prince
38 Facility
39 British pound, informally
40 To the left side of a ship
41 Fleur-de-___
42 Good ol' boy's nickname
43 Comedian Danny of "The Court Jester"
44 Run pledges through the gantlet, say
45 Positive replies
46 Isle of exile for Napoleon
47 English cathedral city
49 ___-friendly
51 Neighborhood
56 Show ___ (Hollywood and such)
58 Fatty bulges
62 Seeped
64 "I smell ___!"

65 Nonglass parts of glasses
66 Martin or McQueen
67 Position
68 Woodwind
69 Person who gives a hoot
70 Miffed, with "off"
71 Neighbor of Wis.

DOWN

1 Home of the Buccaneers
2 Wall-climbing plants
3 Horne and Olin
4 Writer Jong
5 Stupefy
6 Poet ___ St. Vincent Millay
7 Tall tale teller

8 Bawdy
9 Certain acid
10 Homer Simpson's neighbor
11 Singing groups
12 Not imaginary
13 Cry
21 Pieces of ___
22 Sea eagle
26 Brimless hat
28 Kick back
29 Indian corn
30 Good thing to have
32 Barbed remark
33 Nabokov heroine and others
34 Gather leaves
35 "Be ___!" ("Help me out!")
36 Prankster's item
37 Zones

42 Poet who originated the phrase "truth is stranger than fiction"
44 Submarine
48 Thrilled to death
50 Church V.I.P.
52 Modern multimedia tool
53 Accused's need
54 Wretched car
55 City on the Ruhr
56 Popular pear
57 Infinitesimal amount
59 Infinite
60 Lake that feeds Niagara Falls
61 Abhor
63 Apple picker

16

by Rich Norris

ACROSS

1. Automobile pioneer
5. Baby's affliction
10. Sailing maneuver
14. Pub missile
15. "Is that ___?" ("Really?")
16. Precollege, briefly
17. Military attire
19. Iranian money
20. Reggae relative
21. Yarn maker
22. Troutlike fish
23. Plants with small, fragrant flowers
27. Kind of lantern
29. Playwright O'Casey
30. Masters and Jonson, e.g.
31. Pellet propeller
35. Jerk
36. ___ the good
38. Sportscaster Berman
39. One of the Virgin Islands
42. On the ___ (not working)
44. Sign
45. Go along with
47. Leafy dish
51. Willow twig
52. One of the "back 40"
53. Motorists' org.
56. "Scat, cat!"
57. Breakfast side dish
60. Computer list
61. Cow of note
62. Anniversary, e.g.
63. Kiln
64. Check writer
65. Potato features

DOWN

1. Lotto info
2. Escapade
3. Most marvelous
4. Ave. crossers
5. Mountain retreats
6. Recently
7. Actress San Giacomo
8. Diamonds, to a yegg
9. Pennies: Abbr.
10. End points
11. 1979 sci-fi classic
12. Classroom supply
13. Glasgow garb
18. Turns sharply
22. Fight, but not for real
24. It borders four Great Lakes: Abbr.
25. "___ me?"
26. Pianist Peter
27. Calculating types
28. Welcomer
31. Capp and Capone
32. Takes to the air
33. Riga native
34. Auto maker Ferrari
36. New World abbr.
37. Get, as a job
40. Finish putting
41. Bridge expert Sharif
42. Less restrained
43. Cartoon canine
45. Comic strip redhead
46. Big name in baby food
47. Kramer of "Seinfeld"
48. Actor Milo
49. Club members since 1917
50. Given to gabbing
54. What's required to be "in"
55. "___ Death" (Grieg work)
57. Wise
58. It goes before carte, but not horse
59. Keats creation

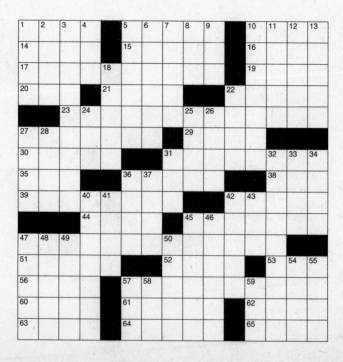

by Gregory E. Paul   17

ACROSS
1 Polish's partner
5 Silents actress Normand
10 Disappearing phone feature
14 Busy person's list heading
15 "The Barber of Seville," e.g.
16 Loafing
17 Dreadful end
18 Hornswoggle
19 Butcher's stock
20 Short-lived success
23 Skull
24 Building wing
25 Skirt fold
28 Second-stringer
31 Command to Bowser
35 Windpipe, e.g.
37 Spigot
39 Not worth a ___
40 Backstabber
44 6–3, in tennis
45 Letter before "cue"
46 Forewarns
47 Crumble, as support
50 Any planet
52 Analyze
53 "Independence Day" invaders
55 Farm fraction
57 Old fogy
63 Trendy
64 Die down
65 Sombrero feature
67 One of six for a hexagon
68 x, mathwise
69 Liquid rock
70 Profess
71 Perfect places
72 Enthusiasm

DOWN
1 The usual: Abbr.
2 [It's gone!]
3 False god
4 Hiawatha's weapon
5 Coffee shop order
6 Plant pests
7 Existed
8 The "E" in Q.E.D.
9 Carpenter's machine
10 Feature of a baby face
11 The very notion
12 TV's Thicke
13 "___ Me Call You Sweetheart"
21 Caterpillar hairs
22 North Pole toymaker
25 Old hat
26 The Titanic, e.g.
27 Muse of poetry
29 Out-and-out
30 Old-fashioned "Phooey!"
32 Russian royals
33 ___ Rica
34 Impudent girl
36 Kennel sound
38 Black-eyed ___
41 Prefix with colonial
42 Blinding light
43 Look like
48 Salt, e.g.
49 And so on, for short
51 Close securely, with "down"
54 Rollerblade
56 Deep Blue's game
57 Switchblade
58 Ocean motion
59 Footnote abbr.
60 Christen
61 Russia's ___ Mountains
62 Beverly Sills, e.g.
63 Civil War letters
66 Million ___ March

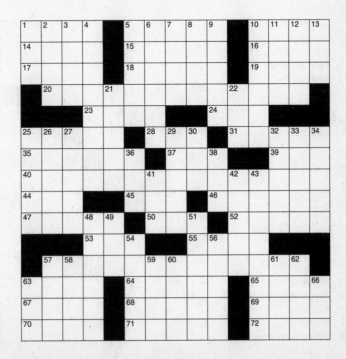

18

by Arthur S. Verdesca

ACROSS

1. Arctic dweller
5. Cuneiform stroke
10. "Pronto!"
14. Treaty signer
15. About the line of rotation
16. 200-meter, e.g.
17. Onetime feminine ideal
20. Big chunk of a drug company's budget
21. Golf's ___ Cup
22. Same old, same old
23. Release money
25. Strait of Dover port
29. Novelty singing feature
33. Modern surveillance tool
34. Actress Winslet
35. Certain theater, for short
36. 1941 Lillian Hellman play
40. Barely make, with "out"
41. Wine sediment
42. Big name in stationery
43. Insane
46. Incenses
47. Filly, e.g.
48. "What's more . . ."
49. ___ Park, N.J.
52. Sun circler
57. Anthony Burgess thriller, with "A"
60. Et ___
61. Foreign
62. Nonplus
63. Emperor in "Quo Vadis?"
64. Primed
65. After-dinner drink

DOWN

1. Cowardly Lion portrayer
2. Cream ingredient
3. "Not only that . . ."
4. Combustible pile
5. Bewhiskered creature
6. On the money
7. Menu offering
8. Xenon, for one
9. Pixie
10. Having a diamond-shaped pattern
11. 50's–60's Mideast king
12. A lot of lot
13. Equal
18. Showy
19. Showy flower
23. Spa
24. On the sheltered side
25. Sounded crowlike
26. Suffering from insomnia
27. Subsequently
28. N.C. State's athletic org.
29. Doomed
30. Stale
31. Drift
32. Uncaps
34. Prepare to be knighted
37. Gymnast Korbut
38. Provide
39. Witch
44. 1955 merger
45. Out-of-the-way place
46. "Friends, Romans, countrymen" orator
48. Begged
49. Shoemaker Thom
50. Lui's partner
51. Film ___
52. Song for Carmen
53. Hoof smoother
54. Aware of
55. Helicopter pioneer Sikorsky
56. Educ. or H.U.D., e.g.
58. Gulf ___
59. Ring cheer

ACROSS

1 Presidential caucus state
5 Relax
9 "The ___ Ranger"
13 Some of it is junk
14 Go ___ detail
15 Rescued
16 French 101 infinitive
17 Croaker
18 Revise
19 1986 Newman/ Cruise movie
22 Site of a ship's controls
23 Debtor's note
24 One-named comedian with a talk show
28 Chaos
32 Like a stadium crowd
33 Stewpot
35 ___ Grande
36 Cynical foreign policy
40 Earnings on a bank acct.
41 Lemon and lime drinks
42 Commie
43 Sites of lashes
46 Pressure
47 "Are you a man ___ mouse?"
48 Landlocked African country
50 "Fiddler refrain"
58 Up and about
59 TV's talking horse
60 Comfort
61 Fred's dancing partner
62 Not yours
63 Cake finisher
64 Carol
65 Picnic invaders
66 Library byword

DOWN

1 "___ a man with seven wives"
2 Sworn word
3 Telegram
4 Actor Guinness
5 Ransacked
6 Register, as for a course
7 Tempest
8 Like some restaurant orders
9 Hope/Crosby costar Dorothy
10 Kiln
11 State bird of Hawaii
12 Whirlpool
15 Pago Pago's land
20 John who wrote "Butterfield 8"
21 Last
24 "Sexy" lady of Beatles song
25 Certain humor
26 Actor Nick
27 ___ Harbour, Fla.
28 Swiss heights
29 Construction site sight
30 Rubes
31 They're used in walking the dog
33 Bettor's stat
34 Golf position
37 Traffic tool
38 Kind of nerve
39 Russian space station
44 Massachusetts city
45 "Goodnight" girl of song
46 Playground equipment
48 California county
49 "___ You Glad You're You?" (1945 hit)
50 Persia, today
51 Pooch's name
52 "Gotcha"
53 Austen heroine
54 Legatee
55 Riot spray
56 Sailing
57 Uncool sort

20

by Elizabeth C. Gorski

ACROSS

1 Front-line chow, once
5 Observer
10 Neighbor of Libya
14 Ear part
15 Fall color
16 In vigorous health
17 Scores on a serve
18 1996 film for which Geoffrey Rush won Best Actor
19 Chester Arthur's middle name
20 Start of a thought by Oscar Wilde
23 Neither's partner
24 Good Housekeeping award
25 Diddley and Derek
28 From the jungle
31 Brew vessels
35 Conductor Klemperer
37 Cozy corner
39 Iron bar
40 Part 2 of the thought
43 New Testament king
44 Flute part
45 Part of Q.E.D.
46 "Gunsmoke" star
48 Back-to-school mo.
50 Peter, Paul and Mary: Abbr.
51 Sleep phenomena
53 Flight
55 End of the thought
63 Up to it
64 Followed a coxswain's orders
65 Kind of miss
66 Safe deposit box item, perhaps
67 Witch
68 Great-great-grandson of Augustus
69 When the French fry?
70 Carved
71 Annexes

DOWN

1 Wooden piece
2 Little of Verdi?
3 Genesis brother
4 A quark and an antiquark
5 90's fashion accessory
6 ___ Rios, Jamaica
7 Waiflike
8 Birds at sea
9 Brand of peanut butter cup
10 Dare
11 Fair share, maybe
12 Jai ___
13 Game rooms
21 "I'll never do it again," e.g.
22 Dine at home
25 South African politico
26 Multiple-choice answer
27 Unsmiling
29 Clark's interest
30 Do's and ___
32 Stravinsky et al.
33 Yogurt type
34 R.B.I.'s and such
36 Wind player's purchases
38 Locale for a spanking
41 Ford flub
42 Blew inward
47 Buss
49 Scot's topper
52 Entrap
54 Food from heaven
55 Stow, as cargo
56 Sarcastic response
57 ___ Bailey
58 Increase
59 Québec's Lévesque
60 "___ I say more?"
61 Joker, e.g.
62 Love's inspiration

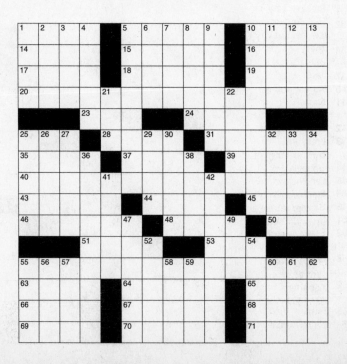

ACROSS

1 More than dislike
6 Big name in computer games
10 Fish from Dover
14 Be loud, as a radio
15 Cawer
16 Let ___ a secret
17 Write without a single mistake
20 Cosmonauts, by definition
21 Perfume essence
22 Phone no. at the office
23 Letters starting naval carrier names
25 With 28-Down, a university in Dixie
26 Cass Elliot was one of them
30 Watering holes
31 Kimono sashes
32 1961 Best Actor Maximilian
34 British rule in colonial India
37 Not play it safe
40 Ave. crossers
41 Nal, e.g., chemically
42 Poems of praise
43 Look surreptitiously
44 Search
45 Prefix with cycle
48 6-pt. scores
49 Sigma follower
51 Spotted pony
53 Sunrise and sunset locales
58 O.K.
61 Sea eagle
62 First number in season records
63 French pupil
64 High schooler
65 Like custards
66 Called one's bluff

DOWN

1 Shortened form, in shortened form
2 ___ cheese dressing
3 Dutch artist Frans
4 Mined metals
5 Knots again
6 Bloodhound's trail
7 Goofs
8 Opposition for Dems.
9 Wonderment
10 Refine, as flour
11 "And ___ grow on"
12 Hometown-related
13 ___ nous
18 I.R.S.'s share
19 Grapple (with), colloquially
23 Overturn
24 Soothing ointment
26 Swabs
27 Adjoin
28 See 25-Across
29 Baseball wood
30 Valentino title role, with "the"
32 Covered the foot
33 Yields
34 Went on horseback
35 King Kong and others
36 It's said with a poke in the ribs
38 First-rate
39 Cardinals great Brock
44 In sets of 24 sheets
45 Come-from-behind victory
46 Saltpeter: Brit.
47 Silly
49 She said "I 'spect I growed"
50 Dadaism founder
52 Govt. agents
53 Be suspended
54 French novelist Émile
55 "Roger, ___ and out!"
56 Central church area
57 Winter toy
59 Be indebted to
60 Not worth a ___

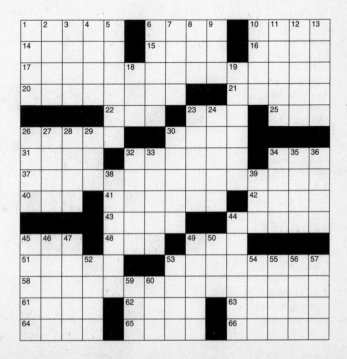

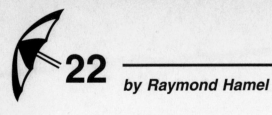

22

by Raymond Hamel

ACROSS
1 Legally impedes
7 May school event, often
11 Like 1, 3, or 7
14 Filled with the old school spirit
15 The last Mrs. Chaplin
16 By way of
17 ST
20 Spreading tree
21 Legal offense
22 Main bloodline
23 Hair division
24 Pharmaceutical-approving org.
25 TU
33 Cut dramatically
34 Not quite closed
35 Life force, in Eastern philosophy
36 Luke's mentor, in "Star Wars"
37 Bombastic
39 Bunny's tail
40 When repeated, a dance
41 Bulging earthenware vessel
42 Legal setting
43 UV
47 Toward the tiller
48 Meadow murmurs
49 Jellied dish
52 Young seal
54 Sign of success
57 VW
60 Little ___, 60's singer
61 Disney's "___ of the South"
62 Runoff point
63 Actress Susan
64 Tarzan's home
65 Canine covering

DOWN
1 Highlands tongue
2 Political comic Mort
3 Relative of Geo. and Robt.
4 Hart Trophy winner, 1970–72
5 1987 Wimbledon winner
6 Steinhauer of the L.P.G.A.
7 Sonnet, e.g.
8 Teased mercilessly
9 Switch settings
10 El toro's opponent
11 Completed
12 Weight loss plan
13 Spreadsheet numbers
18 Silents star Naldi
19 Speckled horse
23 Leaning Tower's city
24 Come apart at the seams
25 Course in which to study Freud
26 Wahine's welcome
27 Kind of beacon
28 Like Fran Drescher's voice
29 What to wear when one goes beddy-bye
30 Come to pass
31 "Star Trek" lieutenant
32 ___-gritty
37 Overabundance
38 The whole enchilada
39 Drunkards
41 Thrown away
42 Johnny Appleseed's real surname
44 Seriously wound
45 "Yeah, sure!"
46 Aplenty
49 Like some cheddar cheese
50 P.G.A. Masters champion Ballesteros
51 Talk in church
52 Go downhill
53 Bigger than the both of us
54 Fat-free, as milk
55 Russo of "In the Line of Fire"
56 Hurler Hershiser
58 Neither's partner
59 Gardner of "The Barefoot Contessa"

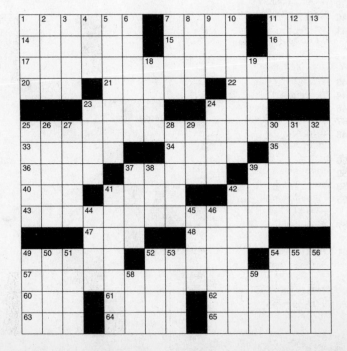

ACROSS

1 "___ Marner"
6 Plopped (down)
9 Luxurious
13 To any degree
14 The Beatles' "___ Love You"
15 French income
16 Prickly plants
17 "Gotcha!"
18 Terminator
19 Train car / Strips again
21 Hooks back up / Winder
23 Chess's ___ Lopez opening
24 Early baby word
25 Time in history
28 Tennis's Sampras
30 Did a no-no / Comics pest
35 Treaty
37 Some paintings
39 Ace plus one
40 Above
41 What each word of six or more letters in this puzzle does
43 Kind of talk
44 Bo of "10"
46 60's singer Sands
47 Pencil filler
48 Writer Hubbard / Grow threefold
50 Sicilian peak
52 Blvds.
53 Profess
55 Opposite of a ques.
57 Security guard / ID at a party
61 No-goodnik / Patches, as a sweater
65 Thunderstruck
66 Without further ___

68 Tropical fruit
69 Dead duck
70 Fish off Nova Scotia
71 Vicinities
72 Squid defenses
73 US Airways competitor
74 West Yorkshire city

DOWN

1 Pouches
2 Type of type: Abbr.
3 Shoestring
4 Do tailoring on
5 Boo-boo / Students
6 Work out in a ring
7 Shade of blond
8 Pageant crown
9 Carson's successor
10 Loosen
11 Dance bit
12 For the woman
15 Newly placed / Telephoner
20 ___ newt (witch's ingredient)
22 Sullivan and Harris
24 Bring to the door / Hugely unpopular
25 Lyric poem
26 "Boléro" composer
27 Sour
29 Scrabble piece
31 Simon or Diamond
32 Art subjects
33 Brilliance
34 Scout's good works

36 Genealogy display
38 Roasting rod
42 French legislature
45 "Seinfeld" guy / Comment
49 Southern power provider: Abbr.
51 "20 Questions" category / Layer
54 Put into effect
56 Entangle
57 1958 musical
58 "Mr. X"
59 Desert Storm vehicle
60 She sheep
61 Fizzy drink
62 On bended ___
63 "Holy moly!"
64 Supreme Diana
67 ___ Jones

24

by Hugh Davis

ACROSS

1 Artist Chagall
5 Words to live by
10 Kind of liquor
14 Coloratura's piece
15 Units to be subdivided
16 ___ vera
17 Water source
18 Financial wherewithal
19 Storm
20 Supermarket tabloid subject #1
23 Fifty-fifty
24 Hosp. procedure
25 Like marble
28 Like Charlie Chan
33 Research facility: Abbr.
34 Policy position
35 Gardner of "Show Boat"
36 Supermarket tabloid subject #2
40 Coach Parseghian
41 Exudes
42 "Stat!"
43 Romeo
45 Cars that are in the shop a lot
47 Hate grp.
48 Donaldson and others
49 Supermarket tabloid subject #3
56 Appear ahead
57 It starts with Genesis
58 Mideast carrier
60 Tulip planting
61 Sans company
62 Rhody, in an old song
63 Concerning
64 More green
65 Lockbox document

DOWN

1 Gullet
2 Geometrician's figuring
3 Brook
4 Hot, in Jalisco
5 "Out, ___ spot!": Lady Macbeth
6 Continental divide?
7 Snag
8 Darn
9 Not checking to make sure
10 1990's Fox sitcom
11 Jai ___
12 Nike's swoosh, for one
13 Popular youth magazine
21 Woman in a garden
22 Words to live by
25 Goldsmith's "The ___ of Wakefield"
26 Start of a new año
27 Faith of five million Americans
28 Playful animal
29 Beams
30 Renaissance Italian poet
31 Birdlike
32 Reindeer herders
34 Judge, with "up"
37 Knocks on the noggin
38 Elton John or Mick Jagger
39 Three-time Masters champ
44 Like some arms
45 Soap (up)
46 Record label inits.
48 Classic 1953 western
49 Isle of exile
50 Reed and Costello
51 Electric unit
52 Seat of Allen County, Kan.
53 Sprout
54 Collagist's need
55 Sensible
59 Inc., abroad

ACROSS

1 Thicket
6 Droop
9 Arguments
14 Month of showers
15 ___-haw
16 Return to base after a fly ball
17 Sentry's position
19 Lyric poem
20 Superlative ending
21 New currency on the Continent
22 Be relevant to
23 Volunteer
25 Central points
29 Genetic letters
30 It might make you say "Aha!"
31 "Aha!"
34 Tour leader
39 Municipal building
42 Nonnational
43 Surf's sound
44 Sorts
45 Lamb's mother
47 Plug's place
49 Quarterback option
55 Bee house
56 Site of Napoleon's first exile
57 Rink surface
60 Lacquer part
61 V.I.P. protector
63 Minotaur's island
64 French article
65 Goaded, with "on"
66 Kind of seal
67 Neighbor of Isr.
68 Flamboyant

DOWN

1 Hamster's home
2 Numbered composition
3 Kind of fall
4 Knight, by definition
5 Firstborn
6 Water's edge
7 "The Lion and the Mouse" writer
8 Receive
9 Cheap ship accommodations
10 Tree with oblong leaves
11 Greek marketplace
12 House style
13 Go on a buying spree
18 Contributes
22 "___ appétit!"
24 Norse love goddess
25 Isinglass
26 Movie star
27 Prefix with god
28 Word said before "time" and "place"
32 Fathered
33 D.D.E.'s command in W.W.II
35 Company part
36 "___ be a cold day . . ."
37 Astronaut Slayton
38 Once, once
40 Like some income on a 1040
41 Stills and Nash partner
46 Twisted
48 Practices
49 You can't take it seriously
50 "The Barber of Seville," e.g.
51 Stair part
52 Actor Ralph of "The Waltons"
53 Flashy flower
54 Birch relative
57 "Othello" villain
58 Airplane staff
59 Small whirlpool
61 Tour transportation
62 "That's horrid!"

26

by Robert Dillman

ACROSS
1 Lady with a title
6 Mirth
10 Evil
13 Carefree song syllables
14 Transport for Huck Finn
15 A large part of Mongolia
16 Stock secretarial ploy #1
19 Catch ___ (start to get)
20 Decorative window shape
21 Artist Max
22 It's baked in a square
24 Strike callers
26 Genteel affair
29 Juices
31 Crones
35 Skylit rooms
37 "Yes, ___!"
38 Command to Dobbin
39 Stock secretarial ploy #2
43 Bingo-like game
44 Pi follower
45 Cockeyed
46 Sharp rebuff
47 It lets off steam
50 Many a Little League coach
51 Seamstress Betsy
53 "___ kleine Nachtmusik"
55 Village smith, e.g.
58 Pantomimist Jacques
60 Meadows
64 Stock secretarial ploy #3
67 Lighten (up)
68 Queen before George I
69 Jaunty
70 Commotion
71 Stink
72 Left one's seat

DOWN
1 Roman emperor in A.D. 69
2 Birdhouse bird
3 Magazine publisher Condé ___
4 "Cats" poet
5 Wasn't colorfast
6 Act servile
7 Turner, the 40's Sweater Girl
8 Offensive smells
9 Beach time in Bordeaux
10 Rhine city
11 Basics
12 Many a New Year's resolution
15 "'S Wonderful" composer
17 Pepsi, e.g.
18 Business solicitor, for short
23 "___ Mommy Kissing Santa Claus"
25 Dramatist Connelly
26 Duties
27 A Barrymore
28 Gladiator's locale
30 "___ the Sheriff" (1974 hit)
32 Leading
33 Slangy word of intention
34 Full, at last
36 Liquid in synthetic rubber manufacture
40 Nettles
41 What witnesses take
42 Mortgage, e.g.
48 Pet restraint
49 CVI halved
52 Cortez's quest
54 Box ___ (tree)
55 Where Dwight Gooden once pitched
56 Principal
57 ___ buco (Italian dish)
59 79 for gold, e.g.: Abbr.
61 Architect Saarinen
62 Inquires
63 Kind of terrier
65 Chinese ideal
66 Health facility

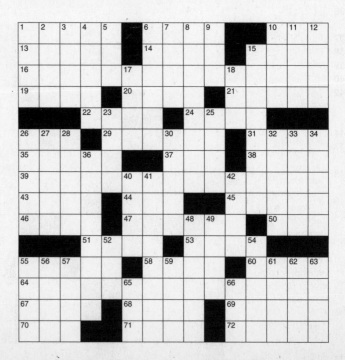

ACROSS

1 "Pow!"
5 Italian sports cars
10 Places for rent: Abbr.
14 Be sore
15 Tennis star Agassi
16 Fox or turkey follower
17 "No way!"
19 Architect Saarinen
20 Busybody
21 Lid decoration?
23 B.&O. and Reading, e.g.: Abbr.
24 Mas' partners
26 The March King
27 "No way!"
31 Bus stations
34 Sneaky scheme
35 Money for old age, for short
36 ___ Stanley Gardner
37 Put in rollers
38 Hosiery problem
39 Woody's ex-mate
40 ___ de vivre
42 Churchill flashed them during W.W. II
44 "No way!"
47 Common sprain spot
48 Gene material, in brief
49 Baby bear
52 One who can see what you're saying
55 Classic Alan Ladd western
57 Jacob's twin
58 "No way!"
60 French seas
61 "No man is an island" poet John
62 Drubbing
63 Clockmaker Thomas
64 Speechify
65 Teachers' favorites

DOWN

1 Nymph chaser
2 Yellowish brown
3 Spots for goatees
4 Clark of The Daily Planet
5 Airline watchdog grp.
6 Eat
7 "An apple ___ . . ."
8 Auditions (for)
9 Light detectors
10 "Relax, private!"
11 Before
12 Matador's threat
13 Put in the overhead rack
18 Finito
22 More than large
25 Complete jerk
27 Slangy coffee
28 Less constrained
29 Teheran's nation
30 Places for prices
31 Moore of "G.I. Jane"
32 Land of the leprechauns
33 Share (in)
37 Delivery entrance, often
38 Bro's counterpart
40 Diner music player, informally
41 Home of Disney World
42 Florist's vehicle
43 Break into smithereens
45 Surge
46 Roving, as a knight
49 It needs a good paddling
50 In its original form, as a movie
51 Red vegetables
52 Moon vehicles
53 Psychiatrist's reply
54 Sicilian spouter
56 Angel's instrument
59 Dee's predecessor

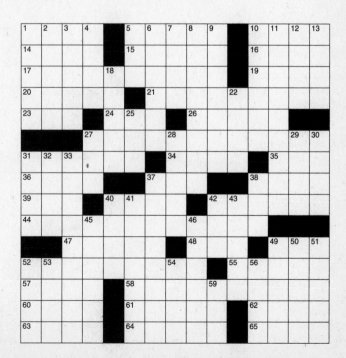

by Janet R. Bender

ACROSS

1 Swiss peaks
5 Sea that's really a lake
9 Morley of CBS
14 Tip seller
15 Paying passenger
16 Florida city
17 Poe writing
18 Washington suburb
20 Mythical strongman
22 Family girl
23 A few coins, in slang
26 Tempe sch.
29 Cool, once
30 Mil. address
31 Botanist Mendel
33 Perfumes
36 Like higher-priced beef
37 You can't enjoy this if you've lost your marbles
42 Ages and ages
43 Dorm room staple
44 Crackpot
47 Was first
48 Ring org.
51 Martians and such
52 Detective with a large family
56 Check (out)
57 Sturm und ___
58 Dog restraint
63 Choir voice
64 Poisoned, for instance
65 Wee, in brief
66 Ardor
67 All tuckered out
68 Female V.I.P.
69 Humorist Bombeck

DOWN

1 Glue (to)
2 Detest
3 Pilot's maneuver
4 Kind of cleaning
5 Steelers' org.
6 Stadium cheer
7 Venue for 48-Across
8 "Deathtrap" playwright
9 World Cup game
10 Pine (for)
11 Org. that keeps an eye on pilots
12 Golfer Ernie
13 Actress ___ Dawn Chong
19 Safecracker
21 Bowler's feat
24 Naval noncoms
25 Realtors' sales
26 Pulitzer winner James
27 Catch the wind under one's wings
28 Cemetery sights
32 Nevada county or its seat
33 Years, to Caesar
34 Do something
35 Beach souvenir
37 Arrived
38 Greenhouse effect?
39 Physics particles
40 ". . . ___ saw Elba"
41 Gave up
45 One way to identify a foreigner
46 Fudge ingredient: Abbr.
48 Capt. Ahab or his ship
49 Big name in paperback publishing
50 Neighbor of Zambia
53 Plant pest
54 Gaucho's rope
55 Mania
56 Trapper's offering
58 Modern records
59 Turning point?
60 Keats's "___ to Psyche"
61 Political subject
62 "Bill ___, The Science Guy"

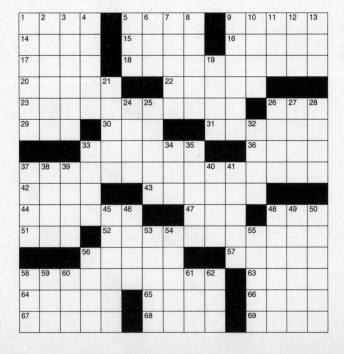

ACROSS

1 "Spare" items at a barbecue
5 Popular athletic shoes
10 Bullets and such
14 Melville tale
15 Beatle with a beat
16 Many a Seattle weather forecast
17 Classic pickup line #1
20 "Six Days, Seven Nights" co-star
21 Early night, to a poet
22 Permit: Abbr.
23 Prefix with -metric
24 Heavy hammer
27 Proofreader's mark
29 Not glossy, as a photo
32 Captain Morgan's drink
33 "Norma ___"
36 Dish served under glass
38 Classic pickup line #2
41 Geometric measurement
42 What Yahoo! searches, with "the"
43 Whichever
44 ___-off coupon
46 Mets stadium
50 Directs (to)
52 Ecol. watchdog
55 The "I" in T.G.I.F.
56 Prefix with skeleton
57 Numbers usually in parentheses
60 Classic pickup line #3
63 Pitcher

64 Genesis woman and namesakes
65 Allen of "Candid Camera"
66 Smart-mouthed
67 Cove
68 Fr. holy women

DOWN

1 Kansas City team
2 "Consider it done"
3 Dribble
4 Achy
5 City where van Gogh painted
6 Broadcasting giant
7 Ruler unit
8 Poet and novelist James
9 Michigan's ___ Canals
10 Napoléon led one
11 Wisconsin Avenue, in Georgetown
12 Opposite of max.
13 Washington's bill
18 ___ Beta Kappa
19 Let go of
24 Uncompromising
25 "Peter ___" of 50's–60's TV
26 Ambulance driver, for short
28 Car on rails
30 To the left, to sailors
31 Fri. preceder
34 Suffered humiliation
35 ___ Park, Colo.
37 Takes a chair
38 Soave, e.g.
39 Spring woe
40 Liking

41 Flag-waving org.
45 Churn
47 Went into seclusion
48 Endless, poetically
49 Liabilities' opposites
51 Put forth, as effort
53 ___ Blue Ribbon
54 Smashing point?
57 "You said it, brother!"
58 Sincere
59 Murders, slangily
60 Cool, once
61 Wonderment
62 ___ Lilly and Company

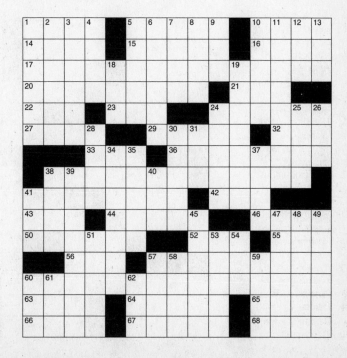

by Randall J. Hartman

ACROSS

1 Droops
5 Hula-Hoops, lava lamps, etc.
9 Tooth trouble
14 24-karat, goldwise
15 Settled down
16 The Sorbonne, e.g.
17 Mediterranean seaport
18 Punjabi peeress
19 Confine
20 Basketball player's credo?
23 Free of charge
24 Blockhead
25 Pindaric work
28 Starchy tuber
29 You, right now
32 Allege as fact
33 Waters
34 Sacramento's Arco ___
35 Soldier's credo?
39 Science fiction, for one
40 "Over the Rainbow" composer Harold
41 "Dragonwyck" author Seton
42 Numb, as a foot
44 Wane
47 Superman foe ___ Luthor
48 Cookout leftover?
49 Armstrong's program
51 Bodybuilder's credo?
54 Worrier's woe, it's said
57 Tickled-pink feeling
58 Quiz show sound
59 "Waterlilies" painter Claude
60 Equipment
61 Prefix with -derm or -therm
62 ___ bear
63 Talks noisily
64 Costner, in "The Untouchables"

DOWN

1 Like foam rubber
2 Display in the night sky
3 Kind of cracker
4 French lawmakers
5 Sends down to the minors
6 Actor Alda
7 Producer De Laurentiis
8 Squelch
9 Fix, as software
10 Environmental sci.
11 "Friends" co-star Courteney
12 He stung like a bee
13 Japanese bread
21 Off-color
22 "___ Town"
25 Finished
26 Say it ain't so
27 Mesozoic or Paleozoic
30 Carol syllables
31 Corruptible
32 Elvis ___ Presley
33 Taj Mahal site
34 Syrian city
35 Hawaiian honker
36 Cameo stone
37 Bauxite or hematite
38 Grain gatherers
39 ___ Friday
42 Nile biter
43 Like a yak's coat
44 "Seinfeld" role
45 Duck hunters' shelters
46 Beatniks beat them
48 Central artery
50 Rhymester Nash
51 Poverty
52 Intestinal sections
53 Minimal high tide
54 "Kill the ___!" (ball park cry)
55 Mauna ___
56 MSNBC rival

ACROSS

1 Help at a heist
5 Calls to a shepherd
9 Deadly
14 Easy gait
15 Qualified
16 Functional
17 Trebek of "Jeopardy!"
18 Spot on a radar screen
19 Fancy British car, informally
20 Walt Disney's first sound cartoon
23 Aria, e.g.
24 Wriggly fish
25 TV adjunct
28 Unbeatable rival
31 Downward bend
34 Lose underpinnings
36 Time delay
37 Catherine ___, wife of Henry VIII
38 Life of the party
42 Pinnacle
43 Mystery writer Deighton
44 Lend-___ Act
45 Shade of blue
46 Late, great crooner
49 Reading room
50 One ___ time
51 Surrounds, with "in"
53 Show girl's suitor
61 Inner circle
62 "Peek-___!"
63 Puerto ___
64 Durant who co-wrote "The Story of Civilization"
65 Singer Braxton
66 List shortener
67 Greenbacks
68 In the public eye
69 Watered-down

DOWN

1 Word of regret
2 Length of fabric
3 Blunted blade
4 Lone Star State
5 Talk nonsensically
6 Flowering
7 Inter ___
8 Labor Day's mo.
9 Avenging spirits of mythology
10 Wake Island, e.g.
11 Cash drawer
12 "___ Do Is Dream of You" (1934 hit)
13 ___-majesté
21 "Waterlilies" painter
22 Consider the pros and cons of
25 Golden Nugget casino locale
26 Stew container
27 Spacious
29 Actress Verdugo
30 Biological container
31 Kind of fork
32 Come to light
33 White House's ___ Room
35 1950's White House monogram
37 Ante-
39 Trojan War epic
40 Fraternity members
41 Site of Crockett's last stand
46 Blue-gray
47 Royal seat
48 Counterreply
50 Jibe
52 Woman with a temper
53 Con game
54 Hawaiian tuber
55 Score after deuce, in tennis
56 Feed bag fill
57 Cousin of a bassoon
58 Nick at ___
59 Org. with eligibility rules
60 The sunny side, in sunny side up

32

by Nancy Salomon

ACROSS

1 Leave without paying
6 Over the edge
10 Not fooled by
14 Group that has its own organ
15 "The Black Stallion" boy
16 Denunciate, with "at"
17 1958 Rosalind Russell comedy
19 As to
20 British sports cars
21 Utopias
22 Dial sounds
23 Plus
24 Like unwashed hair
25 1955 Fred Astaire/ Leslie Caron musical
31 Gardens amidst the sands
32 Left, at sea
33 Photo ___
35 Abbr. on an envelope
36 Free, as knots
37 ___ Alto, Calif.
38 Mink's coat
39 Hankerings
40 Arrived
41 1981 Joan Crawford exposé starring Faye Dunaway
44 Chops (off)
45 "She loves me ___"
46 Clumps of earth
48 Take care of
51 Verse on a vase
54 Throw a tantrum

55 1963 film of a Chekhov classic with Laurence Olivier
57 Word after "roger"
58 Wit Mort
59 Animated Fudd
60 Caution
61 "I" problems
62 Title pages?

DOWN

1 Rip-off
2 Hood
3 They're charged
4 Like a fiddle?
5 Hit 1990's NBC sitcom
6 Clue, for one
7 Money guru Greenspan

8 Precious stones
9 Woodsman's tool
10 Cal Ripken, for one
11 Female butters
12 Spare, maybe
13 Bullfight bravos
18 Whirlpool
22 Pinball foul
23 Yemeni city
24 Very nasty sort
25 It's a fact
26 Reader of heavenly signs
27 Hope of "Peyton Place"
28 Made a choice
29 Ping or zing
30 Challenge for a bowler
31 Bumbling one

34 Junior
36 "Exodus" author
37 Dickinson or Frost, e.g.
39 Ballpark figures
40 Moved to the music, slangily
42 Contemporary
43 Upfront money
46 Meal for the humble?
47 Volcanic flow
48 Barely catch
49 Kind of chamber
50 Building extensions
51 Treater's words
52 Changed colors
53 Pairs with drums
55 Take advantage of
56 Hearty brew

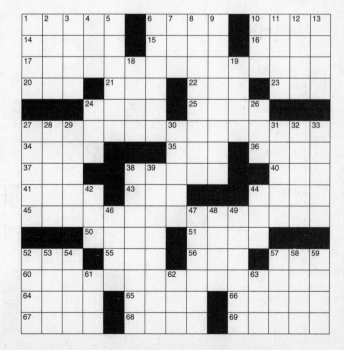

ACROSS

1 Put one's foot down
6 They sometimes accompany photos
10 Onetime Iranian chief
14 Harness racer
15 Answer an invitation
16 Mini's opposite
17 All-out response
20 Criticize, in 90's slang
21 Glimpsed
22 Messenger ___
23 Slalom curve
24 Country north of Chile
25 Tipsy
27 Rich desserts and soap operas, say
34 "Heaven forbid!"
35 Hockey legend Bobby
36 "The World According to ___"
37 Director Jean-___ Godard
38 Having hair like horses
40 Menagerie
41 Monastery titles
43 Aviation hero
44 Alex Trebek, e.g.
45 Jewelry and gold doubloons, maybe
50 Sciences' partner
51 Strived (for)
52 Scottie's bark
55 "Mamma ___!"
56 Time in history
57 Hang on the clothesline
60 Absolutely confident
64 Do as directed
65 River deposit
66 Had title to
67 Treat lavishly
68 P.M. periods
69 Dame Rebecca and others

DOWN

1 Went like the dickens
2 Curbside call
3 Fall mos.
4 Mal de ___
5 Like some stations on a car radio
6 Concoct
7 Any doctrine
8 Rescuee's cry
9 Coronado was one
10 Dallas sch.
11 Tortoise's opponent
12 Chopping tools
13 Snake's warning
18 One of two English queens
19 Gives under pressure
24 Arafat's grp.
26 Warm welcome
27 Does a round of nine
28 Swahili for "freedom"
29 Like an old empire of 24-Across
30 Hermit
31 Gillette product
32 Uneven, as leaves
33 Card markings
38 Decimal part of a logarithm
39 Pretends
42 Music with a blend of folk and calypso
44 1963 Paul Newman film
46 Writer Bombeck
47 Turns inside out
48 Suffix with million
49 Endangered animal in Florida
52 Beginning
53 Hick
54 Guitar part
57 Actress Sothern et al.
58 Skeptic's comment
59 Marge Schott's team
61 It takes in the sights
62 Final: Abbr.
63 Amazement

34

by Randy Sowell

ACROSS

1 Web surfer's need
6 Gulf war foe
10 Moola
14 Levi's "Christ Stopped at ___"
15 In ___ (undisturbed)
16 Iris's place
17 "Eat hearty!"
18 Play opener
19 Puppies' plaints
20 Clotheshorses
23 106, to Caesar
25 Bit
26 Booby trap
27 Harsh conditions
29 See 33-Across
32 Earthy hue
33 With 29-Across, "Barbarella" star
34 ___ Na Na
37 Signal receivers
41 Soon-to-be grads: Abbr.
42 Noted lithographer
43 Finland, to the Finns
44 Rocky rival Apollo ___
46 Tar pits locale
47 Put on, as glue
50 Tinker or Evers or Chance
51 C & W channel
52 Common tabloid topics
57 Artificial bait
58 Led Zeppelin's genre
59 Grinned from ear to ear
62 "Right on!"
63 Shot, e.g.
64 Relaxed
65 Sermon passage
66 Suds
67 Colorado ski resort

DOWN

1 Club ___
2 "Shogun" apparel
3 Sopwith Camel/ Fokker clashes
4 Lamb's "Essays of ___"
5 Old-time trouper
6 "Why? Because ___ so!"
7 "Little Caesar" role
8 Envelope abbr.
9 Witty remark
10 Neighbor of Suriname
11 Title role for Madonna
12 Shunned one
13 Café au lait holder
21 Owns
22 "Acid"
23 Antivampire aid
24 "The ___ of Wakefield"
28 Change from a krone
29 Ill-___ (doomed)
30 Wallet wad
31 Beatty of "Deliverance"
33 Nonsense talk
34 Rizzuto or Reese
35 Macho types
36 Like most Turks
38 "The check is in the mail," perhaps
39 Backer of Columbus
40 Long sandwich
44 Grisham title, with "The"
45 Painter Rembrandt van ___
46 Capt. Jean-___ Picard
47 Key above G
48 Old-fashioned pen
49 Heat-resistant glass
50 "My Fair Lady" director George
53 Snatch
54 A few
55 Zenith
56 Guadalquivir et al.
60 Take advantage of
61 Parker or Waterman

ACROSS

1 Moistureless
5 Feeling for the unfortunate
9 Onetime late-night host Jack
13 Provide with a new soundtrack
15 Nabisco favorite
16 Wheel rod
17 Ice cream flavor #1
20 Vulgarity
21 ___ Lee cakes
22 Neither masc. nor fem.
24 "Too many cooks spoil the broth," e.g.
28 Ice cream flavor #2
33 Model airplane wood
34 Team at Shea
35 Massachusetts' Cape ___
36 Ad-___ (improvises)
37 Mocks
39 Sewing case
40 Brew
41 Grab hold of
42 $1.09 a dozen, say
43 Ice cream flavor #3
47 Mister, in México
48 Argue (with)
49 Faddish 90's collectibles
52 Cause for a blessing?
56 Ice cream flavor #4
61 Merle Haggard's "___ From Muskogee"
62 G.M. or MG product
63 Safe investment, informally
64 Gardener's problem
65 Keep, as cargo
66 Any day now

DOWN

1 Comet's path
2 20's–30's cars
3 Someone who's looked up to
4 North Carolina school
5 Charlatan
6 Lyricist Gershwin
7 Change for a twenty
8 "Star Wars" sage
9 Independence Day event
10 Pink-slip
11 Pie ___ mode
12 Rock group with the 1994 #1 album "Monster"
14 Environmental activist Jagger
18 Book before Daniel: Abbr.
19 Shelled critters
23 Fools (with)
25 Frigid
26 Chronic complainer
27 Singer Gormé
28 Person who holds property in trust
29 Popular catalogue company
30 Buffoon
31 "Do you get it?"
32 A TD is worth 6 of these
33 Down-in-the dumps feeling, with "the"
37 Boxer's punch
38 Wanted poster abbr.
39 Directional suffix
41 Spasm of pain
42 Least tainted
44 Made a better offer than
45 "Strangers and Brothers" novelist
46 Throw a tantrum
50 Mardi ___
51 Porn
53 Sicilian spouter
54 Jerusalem's Mount ___
55 Opposite of endo-
56 Comic book punch sound
57 Make (out)
58 Item for Little Jack Horner
59 Judge Lance ___
60 Barbie's beau

by Gene Newman

ACROSS

1 Book jacket part
5 Admonition to Fido
9 Preserves, as pork
14 Lawn care product
15 Feel the ___
16 Send via cyberspace
17 At the summit of
18 "Dirty" game
19 Bad, as weather
20 Composer on a spree?
23 Nairobi native
24 Land, as a fish
27 Baubles
31 Grp. with a lot of pull?
32 1973 World Series stadium
35 Crucifix inscription
36 Hilo feast
37 Disguise oneself as a composer?
40 Mont Blanc's locale
41 Utah ski spot
42 She loved Narcissus
43 British suffix with American
44 Quadrennial candidate Harold
46 Pesto seasoning
48 Taoism founder
53 Composer's personal attendant?
57 Baby deliverer
59 Raindrop sound
60 Robin Cook novel
61 Find the value of x
62 Points (at)
63 "Redemption" author
64 Dirty political tactic
65 Wear a long face
66 Wine choice

DOWN

1 Back pocket liquor bottle
2 Loose-limbed
3 "___ for the Misbegotten" (O'Neill play)
4 Full of energy
5 On one's back
6 1982 Disney film
7 Bug-eyed
8 Cheerleader's cheer
9 Has a hunch
10 Stun
11 Ultimate satisfaction, in a way
12 Small bird
13 Like a fox
21 Polytheistic
22 Professor Corey
25 State with a panhandle
26 Seagoing: Abbr.
28 Novelist Cather
29 Flying pests
30 Puccini pieces
32 Tortilla chip topper
33 "I could eat a horse," e.g.
34 Asner and Bradley
36 Driver's need: Abbr.
37 Secretary of State under Reagan
38 Flat fixer
39 French legislature
44 More disgusted
45 Pass by
47 Caterpillar or grub
49 Come about
50 From top to bottom, informally
51 Teamsters' wheels
52 Wipe out
54 W.W. II fare
55 Award for Saatchi & Saatchi
56 Frolic
57 Snaky sound
58 Mr. Turkey

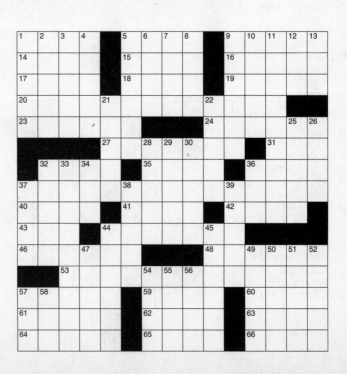

ACROSS

1 Toasted sandwiches, for short
5 Politician Alexander
10 Very funny one
14 Dublin's land
15 Habitation
16 The "I" in "The King and I"
17 Send out
18 Suppers
19 Hoof it
20 Agitated
23 Caustic substance
24 Mrs. Kowalski, in "A Streetcar Named Desire"
25 Hall-of-Famer Yogi
27 1950's car with a horse-collar grille
30 Yak, yak, yak
33 Buffoons
36 "The Wind in the Willows" character
38 World leader who gave his name to a jacket
39 Zilch
40 Browbeat
42 Trains to the Loop
43 Bring out
45 Fodder holder
46 Lose sleep (over)
47 Harbor a grudge about
49 Frisco gridder
51 Softens, with "down"
53 Golf shoe features
57 Word repeated in "Does ___ or doesn't ___?"
59 Agitated
62 Prayer receiver, with "the"
64 Sweater size
65 Neck hair

66 Comply
67 Turn outward
68 Tommie of the 60's–70's Mets
69 Portend
70 "Walk Away ___" (1966 hit)
71 Brainy, socially inept sort

DOWN

1 Strengthens, with "up"
2 See 56-Down
3 Said too often
4 Pays, as a bill
5 Chew out
6 Have ___ in one's bonnet
7 Castle defense
8 Wing it, speechwise

9 Visited again
10 Inexperienced
11 Agitated
12 "Members ___"
13 Give's partner
21 Long in the tooth
22 Guzzled
26 I-95, e.g.: Abbr.
28 Seemingly forever
29 Rabbit fur
31 Writer ___ Stanley Gardner
32 Reddish-brown
33 Lulu
34 Candy striper, e.g.
35 Agitated
37 Takeout lunch provider
40 Redhead's secret, maybe
41 Basement floor material

44 Corp. numero uno
46 One released from bondage
48 Bank employee
50 Antlered animal
52 Work like a dog
54 "If it ain't broke, don't fix it," e.g.
55 Radio part
56 With 2-Down, 65 miles per hour, say
57 Hardly a neatnik
58 Tramp
60 Songbird
61 Fearsome one
63 Hair coloring

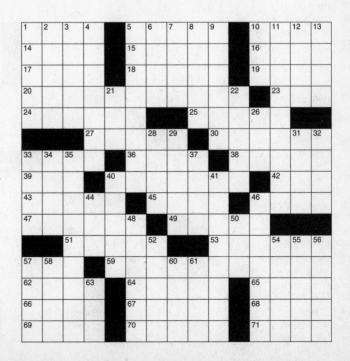

38

by Nancy Salomon

ACROSS
1 Volcano flow
5 Kind of drum or fiddle
9 Halloween disguises
14 Passing notice
15 Get sore
16 Tatum or Ryan
17 Makeup brand
19 Join forces
20 French farewell
21 March of ___
23 Nada
24 Ran first
25 Accountant's software
28 Porterhouse or T-bone
29 Many a Melville setting, with "the"
30 They may be served with a twist
33 Pork cut
37 Like some pre-Columbian culture
38 Golden attribute?
41 Filmdom's Joel or Ethan
42 Removes gently
43 Home of the Bears and the Bulls: Abbr.
46 Exhibit annoying satisfaction
47 Silky-haired dog
51 Pvt.'s boss
54 Little piggy?
55 Skater Hamilton
56 Wedding seater
58 Full of chutzpah
60 End-of-filming gala
62 See eye to eye
63 Bit of Italian bread?
64 Verne's captain
65 Exams
66 1974 Sutherland/Gould spoof

67 Broadway star Verdon

DOWN
1 The slo-o-o-ow train
2 Dwelling
3 Lively, as an imagination
4 Suit to ___
5 Grocery tote
6 Harmful precipitation
7 Screams
8 Alabama march city
9 Puddinglike dessert
10 ___ Arbor, Mich.
11 Take by force
12 Couric of "Today"

13 "George Washington ___ here"
18 Rural
22 Asner and Begley
26 Baseball's Tony or Alejandro
27 Most hearty
28 Horrid smell
30 Computer that doesn't use Windows
31 ___ dye (chemical coloring)
32 Way to go: Abbr.
34 Mrs. Lennon
35 Hosp. section
36 After-tax amount
38 Healthful
39 "Time ___ My Side" (Stones hit)

40 Precede, with "to"
42 Swellhead's journey?
44 Corned beef dishes
45 Co. abbr.
47 Chance for a hit
48 Smithy
49 First, second, reverse, etc.
50 Bays, in a way
51 Chronic nag
52 "___ to the Church on Time"
53 Don at the tailor's
57 Crooned
59 Put in rollers
61 Mas' mates

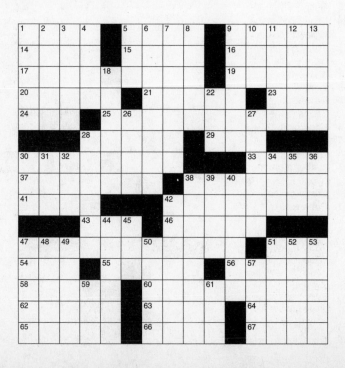

ACROSS

1 Money in a wallet
5 Playbill listing
9 "Pooh!"
14 Elbow-wrist connection
15 Mixed bag
16 Florida city
17 Down under toy
19 Comedian Richard
20 Finalize, with "up"
21 Prefix with cycle
22 Bears witness (to)
24 Country west of Togo
26 "___ do you do?"
27 Make the rounds in a police car
30 Haphazardly
35 Assumed name
36 Unseal
37 Russo of "Ransom," 1996
38 Barbecue entree
39 What each of the four long answers in this puzzle is
40 Dewrinkle
41 Nights before
42 Brainbusting
43 Par ___ (airmail label)
44 Oust from authority
46 Droopy-eyed
47 Engine need
48 Part of a flight
50 Russian plain, with "the"
54 Wane
55 Place for a plane
58 ___ diem (seize the day): Lat.
59 Upgrade from a tropical storm
62 Flying saucer flier
63 Diarist Frank
64 District

65 Molson's and Coors, e.g.
66 Rolling stones lack it
67 Place for a fisherman

DOWN

1 Chicago nine
2 Burn balm
3 The "white" of "White Christmas"
4 Western omelet ingredient
5 Place to break a bronco
6 Actor Delon
7 Kind of tax
8 Roman robe
9 Soda-can opener
10 Tool belt item

11 Makes bales of alfalfa
12 Zillions
13 Battles
18 Community spirit
23 Express gratitude to
24 Singing insect
25 Has hopes
27 Skinned
28 ___ and kicking
29 Dalai Lama's land
31 Borrow's opposite
32 Mountaintop home
33 Meddle
34 Funnyman Youngman
36 Algerian port of 600,000
39 Wild Asian dog
43 Accused's excuse
45 Matures

46 Buffalo's N.H.L. team
49 Sea swallows
50 Sign of healing
51 Saga
52 New York's ___ Canal
53 Hoax
55 Madras dress
56 Spoon-playing site
57 2001, e.g.
60 Lively card game
61 Spending limit

40

by Gilbert H. Ludwig

ACROSS

1 Green stuff
6 On ___ (without assurance of payment)
10 Fivesome on a five
14 Kind of committee
15 Spanish snack
16 Org. protecting workers
17 "Some Like It Hot" co-star
19 Innocent
20 Like a hit B'way show
21 Mex. neighbor
22 Filler of holes
24 Make ___ for it
25 Mrs. Addams, to Gomez
26 1990's boxing champion
31 Fairly
32 Actor Cariou
33 Little worker
35 Worker's demand
36 Bro's kin
37 Housing unit
39 Extra-play periods: Abbr.
40 Essen exclamation
41 TV cop Chris
42 Country star who sang "Roses in the Snow"
46 "Othello" role
47 Commedia dell'
___
48 Level, in taxes
51 Columnist Marilyn ___ Savant
52 Triangular sail
55 Music genre since the 50's

56 Onetime winner of all the awards in this puzzle's theme
59 Raison d'___
60 Privy to
61 Intensely hot
62 Treat for Little Miss Muffet
63 Taj Mahal city
64 Ruffled

DOWN

1 They may be left at one's doorstep
2 Whiff
3 "Curses!"
4 Actress Myrna
5 On target
6 Leave high and dry
7 Frisk, with "down"

8 Formal correspondence
9 Sea north of Iran
10 Blanket wrap
11 Writer Dinesen
12 Rizzuto or Collins
13 Protected
18 Great deal of interest
23 Blonde shade
24 Takes steps
26 Take to the soapbox
27 Earthquake
28 Friend of Job
29 One-named New Age musician
30 Aconcagua and environs
31 Old hand
34 Trifle
36 Darting

37 Hauls away
38 Grimm figure
40 Camus's birthplace
41 Rebound shot
43 It's a knockout
44 Jabber
45 Castro's capital
48 Suds
49 "Portnoy's Complaint" author
50 Bit of a spread
52 Minced oath
53 Start of a legal memo
54 "Cheers" bartender Woody ___
57 Rocky peak
58 Estuary

ACROSS

1 Actor Baldwin
5 Will-o'-the-wisp locale
10 Peninsula south of California
14 Watch face
15 Bone below the femur
16 Satanic
17 Prefix with -nautics
18 Top talent
19 ___ Strauss & Co.
20 Test type
23 Sacred
24 WSW's opposite
25 Cowlike
28 Disaster often not covered by insurance
33 Sports event site
34 ". . . bombs bursting ___"
35 Doctors' org.
36 Anthem
37 Possible answers for 20-Across
38 Proverbial inheritors
39 ___ nutshell
40 Fine china
41 Andrew Wyeth's "___ Pictures"
42 Come crashing down
44 Astronomical object with a large red shift
45 It's south of Eur.
46 Heaven's Gate, e.g.
47 D, often
54 Prod
55 Flu cause
56 Too
57 Good luck symbol for King Tut
58 "You ___ kidding!"

59 Animal with a mane
60 Mediocre
61 Soup onions
62 Cuts with garden shears

DOWN

1 Actor Baldwin
2 Stead
3 Viscount's superior
4 Duds
5 Paper clip alternative
6 "Free" whale of film
7 Irish Rose's guy
8 Odds and ends: Abbr.
9 Terribly weak, as an excuse
10 Dogma

11 With: Fr.
12 Jazz talk
13 ___ Baba
21 Island of the Inner Hebrides
22 ___ about (approximately)
25 Acronymic computer language name
26 Maine college town
27 Open to bribery
28 One place to hook up the jumper cables
29 Give a hoot
30 Scottish Highlanders
31 Symbol of resistance
32 Capital of Senegal
34 Nigerian natives

37 "Thumbs up" signification
38 Spaghetti topper
40 Sound's partner
41 Dance done in grass skirts
43 Crow's-nest cry
44 Grand searches
46 Solid portion
47 Naughty deed
48 Acorn sources
49 Order after "aim"
50 Logic diagram
51 Hodgepodge
52 Initials on a brandy bottle
53 Incalculable amount of time
54 Tank filler

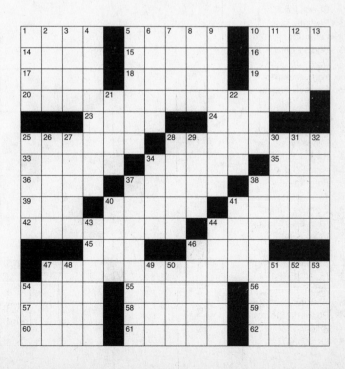

42

by Nancy Salomon

ACROSS

1 Part of P.T.A.: Abbr.
5 Make sense
10 St. Thomas or St. Martin
14 It's hard for some people to carry
15 Dough
16 N.Y. Met or L.A. Dodger, e.g.
17 White's dessert?
19 Fly high
20 Ho hello
21 Dried up
22 There's no free ride on these hwys.
23 Key task?
25 Fable fellow
27 "Row, Row, Row Your Boat" and others
30 Check for fit
33 Prepare for a rainy day
36 Bud's buddy
37 Disco spinner
38 Prop in slapstick
39 Carrey's snack food?
41 Mine find
42 Shows flexibility, in a way
44 Hit like Holyfield
45 Numero uno
46 Free-for-all
47 Western howler
49 Blender maker
51 Like Joe Average
55 From pillar to ___
57 Televises
60 Bid the bed adieu
61 ___ in a blue moon
62 Sawyer's beef?
64 Sharif of "Doctor Zhivago"
65 Leg bone
66 Life-or-death matter: Abbr.
67 The lady's
68 Like snakeskin
69 Madams' men

DOWN

1 Trip to the plate
2 Rude and sullen
3 Be a busybody
4 Recently employed worker
5 Diplomat: Abbr.
6 Bucks' mates
7 Fuss over, with "on"
8 Extremists
9 Check casher
10 Coming up
11 Pesci's sandwich?
12 Faucet failure
13 Screws up
18 Billionth: Prefix
24 Patsies
26 Stern's opposite
28 "___ won't be afraid" ("Stand by Me" lyric)
29 Flying elephant
31 They fit in locks
32 Nikita's "no"
33 Junk E-mail
34 Glorified gofer
35 Wilde's entree?
37 Popular pencil brand
39 Let it be, editorially
40 Newborn child, for one
43 Bothers à la baby brother
45 They may be black and blue
47 Siskel or Ebert
48 Warty-skinned critter
50 Bridge positions
52 Home of the N.B.A. Heat
53 "Lou Grant" star
54 Salacious looks
55 Christopher Robin's pal
56 Treater's words
58 Singer McEntire
59 Go yachting
63 Mary ___ of cosmetics

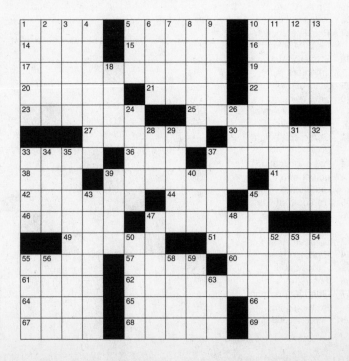

ACROSS
1 The "A" of N.E.A.
5 Vittles
9 Take ___ at (try)
14 Cookout in Honolulu
15 Convenience
16 Hangman's ___
17 Snapshots
18 Perfectly draftable
19 1966 movie or song
20 Judge's query to a jury
23 Army div.
24 Confucian path
25 Muhammad ___
28 Apothecary's weight
31 Sparkly rock
36 Nothin'
38 "___ Coming" (1969 hit)
40 Prom, say
41 Jury's reply to the judge
44 Irregularly edged
45 Word to a fly
46 Pioneering 70's video game
47 ___ Cranston (the Shadow, of old radio)
49 Shoemaker's tools
51 Golf ball prop
52 It lacks refinement
54 ___ Abner
56 Judge's comment to the spectators
65 Actress Adams and others
66 Live wire, so to speak
67 Nile queen, informally
68 Gladiator's battleground
69 More than a goblin
70 German philosopher
71 "Stop worrying!"
72 Prison area
73 Within: Prefix

DOWN
1 Brand for Bowser
2 Make a mess of
3 Diplomat's forte
4 Fish food?
5 Tale spinner Chaucer
6 Rajah's mate
7 Druggie
8 Admirer of Beauty
9 Tight wrapper?
10 Unassisted
11 Bean curd
12 X ___ xylophone
13 Shade of red
21 Stop
22 Dog's ID
25 Broadway backer
26 Classic 1944 mystery film
27 "Going to the dogs," e.g.
29 "Oh, woe!"
30 Baryshnikov, to friends
32 Marshal Wyatt
33 Gold bar
34 Public spat
35 Marsh plant
37 "Not only that . . ."
39 Garbage boat
42 Jazz combo instrument
43 Yelled
48 Prefix with chloride
50 Urge to attack, with "on"
53 Provide with funds
55 English philosopher
56 "The Rubáiyát" poet
57 Stamp designation
58 Hamilton's last act
59 ___ St. Vincent Millay
60 Costume for Claudius
61 Mister, in Münster
62 ___ Bator, Mongolia
63 Monthly money
64 Dog in Oz

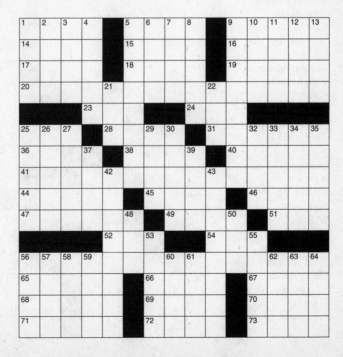

44

by Thomas W. Schier

ACROSS

1 Flashlight's projection
5 Bus. get-together
8 Adjust on the timeline
14 With 2-Down, "My People" author
15 Pacific battle site, in brief
16 Fromm and Remarque
17 Australian ranch hand
19 Lunatics
20 Pyrenees nation
21 Pretty marble
22 Showy parrot
24 Chinese food additive
27 Dali or Corot
28 Mass robe
31 Needed liniment
33 Tot's game
36 Braincases
38 Connect via phone
39 Leaping marsupial
42 Pacific island nation
43 Workout facility
44 Tax on imports
47 Certain M.I.T. grads
48 Cowboy
50 In its entirety
53 Austrian Alpine pass
58 Where 26-Down is
59 Algonquian Indian
60 Donut coatings
61 Drink on draft
62 Peru's capital
63 "Murder Must Advertise" writer Dorothy

64 Tripper's turn-on
65 Like some drinks

DOWN

1 Mexicali locale, for short
2 See 14-Across
3 Alphabetical start
4 Shark variety
5 Medicine chest door, usually
6 Having one intermission
7 Baby syllable
8 Did a framer's job
9 Sappho's Muse
10 Child's reply to a taunt
11 Highest point
12 Unnamed ones
13 Feudal worker

18 Los Angeles suburb
21 Job for Holmes
23 Laotian money
24 Baseball's Connie and others
25 Dump into a dumpster
26 Lake Volta's country
28 Once in ___ moon
29 River through Tours
30 Year-end check, maybe
32 Our lang.
34 Relations
35 Motorists' org.
37 Where nudes may be sketched
40 Tasting like certain wood

41 Man-mouse connector
45 Certain letter-shaped tracks
46 Involuntary, as a landing
48 Pool table fabric
49 Gastric woe
50 Makes "it"
51 "Man ___ Mancha"
52 Caterer's carrier
54 "Road" picture destination
55 Colossal
56 City on seven hills
57 Prod
59 ___ Kan (pet food brand)

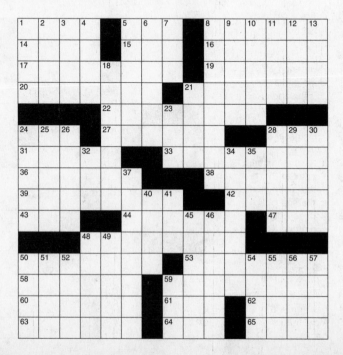

ACROSS

1 Shirking working
5 Wetland
10 Big dud
14 Butter substitute
15 80's–90's singer Baker
16 Not prerecorded
17 Kids' building playthings
19 Prophetic sign
20 Rat fink
21 Private instructors
23 Corrida cry
24 Deep chasm
26 Actress Lollobrigida
28 Wily
29 It gives an artist backing
33 Carson's successor
34 Not mass-produced
36 Santa ___, Calif.
37 Tolkien creatures
38 "Mamma ___!"
39 Queen's subject?
41 Tilt, as the head
42 Oregon's capital
43 Actor Vigoda
44 Excellent, in modern slang
45 "Stars and Stripes Forever" composer
47 "Ben-___"
48 ___ scampi
51 Winnie-the-Pooh's creator
55 Telly Savalas's lack
56 Small telescopes
59 First word in a fairy tale
60 "Silas Marner" novelist
61 Soviet news agency
62 Lyric poems
63 Salad bar servers
64 1988 Olympic gold-medal swimmer Kristin

DOWN

1 Oodles
2 Came down to earth
3 Greek philosopher of paradox fame
4 John Lennon's wife
5 One of the Osmonds
6 Poker player's payment
7 Brazilian city
8 Pigs' digs
9 Rash
10 Ocean debris
11 Car with a bar
12 Out's partner
13 State prisons
18 Grammy winner Fitzgerald
22 Computer operators
24 Poor woodcutter of folklore
25 "Puzzle by Peter Gordon," e.g.
26 Italian salami city
27 Counting everything
28 Israeli natives
30 Neighbor of Fiji
31 Proclamation
32 Breach of secrecy
33 Young woman
34 Gout spot
35 Giant slugger Mel
37 Phrase spoken with a wave into a TV camera
40 Longs for
41 His art is a wrap
44 Mountain lion
46 Win for the underdog
47 Ceases
48 "Git!"
49 Round of applause
50 Houston university
51 Full of excitement
52 Future attorney's exam: Abbr.
53 Hornet's home
54 Old gas brand
57 Arafat's org.
58 Yang's counterpart

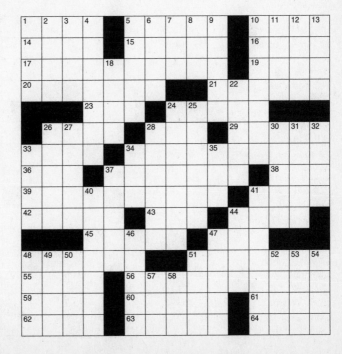

46
by Elizabeth C. Gorski

ACROSS
1 Supreme Diana
5 Distiller Walker
10 Shade of blue
14 1975 Wimbledon winner
15 Solo
16 Plunks (down)
17 Summer resort off the coast of Massachusetts
19 Bring in
20 Elixirs
21 Saviors
23 Ward of "Sisters"
25 D'Amato and others
26 The "S" of R.S.V.P.
29 Elvis's home
33 "At Seventeen" singer Janis
36 Hut material
38 Two socks
39 On a single occasion
40 Scented pouches
43 Quaker's "you"
44 Mine extracts
45 Balance sheet item
46 Make soaking wet
47 Sound systems
49 60's radicals: Abbr.
50 Surgery sites, for short
52 Jugglery
54 Make king
59 Regal headwear
63 Henry ___
64 1984 Prince hit
66 Have ___ good authority
67 Cream
68 Book after II Chronicles
69 Late-night regular
70 Athletic shoe feature
71 Hard to fathom

DOWN
1 Undivided
2 Norse capital
3 Blackball
4 Common carriers
5 Pain in the neck
6 Hurting
7 Wander
8 Author Rice
9 Club ___ (resorts)
10 Blooming time
11 Funny feeling
12 Neighbor of 27-Down
13 Nile creatures
18 Old-time deliverers
22 Carrier to Stockholm
24 Current name
26 Smelling ___
27 The Oregon Trail crossed it
28 Aphrodisiac
30 Cutter
31 Many a snake
32 Recipient of annual contributions
34 Didn't dillydally
35 Hatching places
37 Spell-off
39 Sounds of surprise
41 Precise moment
42 "A Chorus Line" girl
47 Ukr., once
48 Means of release
51 Safari sight
53 Dog-___ (well-worn)
54 Fiendish
55 Evening, in adspeak
56 Intl. acronym since 1960
57 Not valid
58 Toledo's lake
60 Bring the house down
61 Billion follower
62 Ginger cookie
65 Org. looking after kids

ACROSS

1 Modern communication
6 Holland export
10 1944 battle site
14 Where Pago Pago is
15 "La Bohème" heroine
16 One with a look-alike
17 Interpreter of the news
19 Epidemic
20 C.I.A. predecessor
21 "___ Irae" (Latin hymn)
22 Mishandles
24 Soccer great born Edson Arantes
25 "Rob Roy" author
26 The ___ that be
29 Magic charm
32 They're worn on the day after Mardi Gras
33 Dot on a computer screen
34 Sumac whose voice covered five octaves
35 It's dipped in a dip
36 Carpentry grooves
37 Actress Adams of James Bond films
38 Suffix with mountain
39 Respected man
40 Iranian language
41 Soup crackers
43 More subdued
44 Babble
45 Peace symbol
46 Victors' reward
48 Car at an auto dealership
49 ___ Paulo, Brazil
52 Stage accessory
53 Recovery
56 Prisoner's spot
57 Burden
58 Upper crust
59 Church recess
60 Beep on a beeper
61 Frighten off

DOWN

1 Exxon predecessor
2 Guidebook features
3 French friends
4 It's charged in physics
5 Fire truck equipment
6 Host
7 Dah's counterparts
8 Latin 101 word
9 Smokey Robinson's group, with "the"
10 Swaggers
11 "Make me do it"
12 Time Inc. magazine
13 Wallet stuffers
18 Rembrandts, e.g.
23 Seethe
24 Chick's sound
25 Anglo-___
26 Walks a hole in the carpet
27 Actor Milo or Michael
28 Fancy bath features
29 Neap and ebb
30 Make smile
31 Very depths
33 Check casher
36 "Keep going!"
37 Stag attender
39 Clock face
40 Having winning odds
42 Almost a homer
43 Knocked-out state
45 Impenetrable
46 Pet protector, for short
47 Kind of school
48 The "D" of D.E.A.
49 Diamonds, e.g.
50 Chip in
51 Frankfurt's river
54 Spanish article
55 Corrida cry

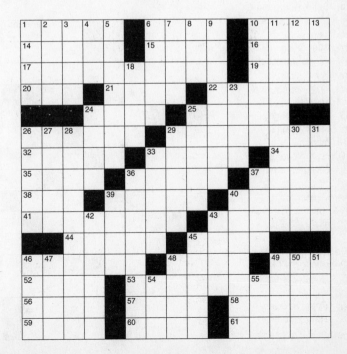

48
by Nancy Salomon

ACROSS
1 Disney's deer
6 With 16-Across, a famed diarist
11 "Am __ believe . . . ?"
14 'Hoods
15 Get a new tenant for
16 See 6-Across
17 Mighty Cardinal
19 __ Cruces, N.M.
20 ". . . sting like __"
21 "Oh wow!"
22 Broken-down motorist's signal
24 Nickname of 17-Across hero Babe Ruth
28 On the train
31 Unbending
32 Gets really steamed
33 Suffix with gang
34 Massachusetts' Cape __
37 Turn loose
39 Official reproach
42 N.F.L. scores
43 Cooperate with a shooter
45 Playful animal
46 Lamb Chop's mentor
48 Had relevance to
49 Call after a hit by 17-Across
53 Minxes
54 "Cara __" (1965 hit)
55 Diva's big moment
59 State next to Miss.
60 Title for 17-Across
64 ". . . __ a lender be"
65 Clear the board
66 Contradict
67 Little scurrier
68 Sees socially
69 Where Minos ruled

DOWN
1 Crimson Tide, briefly
2 Show horse
3 Nothing more than
4 Popular fund-raiser
5 Credo
6 Vernacular
7 1980's sitcom with two Darryls
8 The Greatest
9 Suffix with cash
10 Opponent for Martina or Monica
11 Nonblood relative
12 Princess topper
13 Beginning
18 Common ailment
23 Hallucination cause
25 Constellation bear
26 One in the family
27 Very nasty sort
28 Border on
29 007
30 Squelches a squeak
33 Pint-sized
34 Like a button
35 After-lunch sandwich
36 Actor Bruce
38 Bit of a tiff
40 American-born Queen of Jordan
41 Runner in the raw
44 Kind of cat
46 Pacifier
47 Quite quiet
48 Bridges of Hollywood
49 The Donald's first ex
50 Eagle's gripper
51 Bright
52 Takes on
56 Get to, so to speak
57 "What's __ for me?"
58 Onetime Time film critic James
61 Man-mouse link
62 Welcome __
63 "ER" network

ACROSS

1 "It's a Wonderful Life" director Frank
6 Quiet valley
10 New York Shakespeare Festival founder Joseph
14 Apportion
15 Roof overhang
16 "Hair" song "___ Baby"
17 With 61-Across, what the judge said to the bigamist?
20 Japanese wrestling
21 Your and my
22 Nearly
23 Appear, with "up"
25 At rest
26 Sneeze sounds
29 Casey Jones, notably
33 When repeated, a Latin dance
34 Raison ___
36 Musical composition
37 Put on ___ (act snooty)
39 Peter or Patrick, e.g.
41 "Cut that out!"
42 Smooth and shiny
44 Catch fish, in a primitive way
46 Time in history
47 Modern-day halts to kids' fights
49 "Messiah" composer
51 "You wouldn't ___!"
52 Green flavor
53 Aussie "chick"
56 Dracula, at times
57 "Oh, nonsense!"
61 See 17-Across
64 Elderly's svgs.
65 Caspian Sea feeder
66 "Hi"
67 Defrost
68 "Auld Lang ___"
69 Baby bird

DOWN

1 Low islands
2 Baseballer Matty or Felipe
3 Prune, formerly
4 Highly ornamented style
5 Tell ___ glance
6 Outfit
7 Comic Bert
8 A Gabor
9 State east of the Sierras
10 Easy monthly ___
11 It follows "peek" in a baby's game
12 Name of 12 popes
13 Saucy
18 Hangmen's needs
19 "Dallas" matriarch Miss ___
24 16½ feet
25 "Goodnight" girl of song
26 ". . . with ___ of thousands!" (Hollywood hype)
27 Texas cook-off dish
28 Sultan's ladies
29 Excursions
30 Quiet
31 Be crazy about
32 Where Everest is
35 Nibble on
38 Most flea-bitten
40 Idyllic South Seas island
43 Aussie "bear"
45 Hit head-on
48 Neighbor of Saturn
50 Huey, Dewey or Louie, to Donald Duck
52 Soup server
53 Take some off the top
54 Tortoise's rival
55 List-ending abbr.
56 Noggin
58 "___ be a cold day in hell . . ."
59 Only
60 What 69-Across will grow up to do
62 Arid
63 Nevertheless

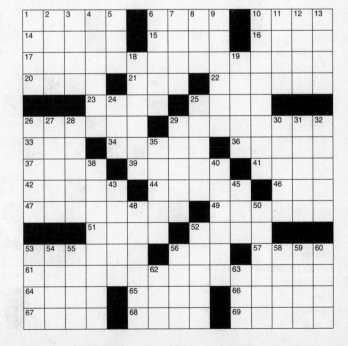

50

by Fred Piscop

ACROSS
1 "Peanuts" boy
6 Exile of 1979
10 Carry on, as a campaign
14 Take for one's own
15 Shells, e.g.
16 Allege as fact
17 With one's fingers in a lake?
20 Grand larceny, e.g.
21 "___ Darlin' " (jazz standard)
22 Sugary drink
23 "Relax, private!"
26 Longed (for)
28 Adorns unnecessarily
31 Toiletries holder
33 Brouhaha
34 A.T.M. necessity
35 Wagnerian heroine
39 With one's fingers in a skyscraper?
43 Like last year's styles
44 Part of U.C.L.A.
45 KLM competitor
46 Echo, e.g.
48 An ex of Xavier
50 Bob Cousy's team, for short
53 Duds
55 "Bravo!"
56 Wax producer
58 Latino lady
62 With one's fingers in a socket?
66 Bering Sea island
67 At no time, to poets
68 Ceramists' needs
69 Element #10

70 City to which Helen was abducted
71 Kind of shooting

DOWN
1 Joke response, informally
2 ___ fixe (obsession)
3 December air
4 Send to a mainframe
5 Is miserly
6 Decline in value
7 Seagoing inits.
8 Evil repeller
9 Pueblo dweller
10 Kind of chest or paint
11 For the birds?
12 Hollow rock

13 Blew it
18 "The Science Guy" on TV
19 Ciudad Juárez neighbor
24 Similar
25 Marathoner's shirt
27 Borodin's prince
28 Meower, in Madrid
29 Matinee hero
30 Blaring
32 0's and 1's, to a programmer
34 Absolute worst, with "the"
36 One of the Simpsons
37 Cherished
38 Sinclair rival
40 Cyberspace conversation
41 Grimm youngster

42 Launderer's step
47 ___ Brothers
48 Haunted house sounds
49 Playwright Ibsen
50 "Over There" composer
51 Make jubilant
52 Slowly, on a score
54 Approximation suffix
57 "___ Too Proud to Beg" (1966 hit)
59 Look at flirtatiously
60 Tennis's Lacoste
61 Like some profs.
63 Pester for payment
64 Prefix with logical
65 Have a bawl

ACROSS

1 Pitcher
5 Egyptian vipers
9 TV's Pyle
14 Lose brilliancy
15 Shed, as skin
16 The "I" of IM
17 Nonstop round-the-clock, informally
20 Clement Moore's "right jolly old elf"
21 Watches for
22 ___ longa, vita brevis
24 Most optimistic
28 NASA's Armstrong
31 Stumped solvers' requests
34 CCLVI doubled
35 California's Fort ___
36 Crunchy sandwich
37 Raison ___
38 Start of a free call
42 Dress lines
43 "No problem!"
44 Not a particular
45 From Santiago to Buenos Aires
46 Cop's ID
48 Actual being
49 Olympian's no-no
51 Boston Red ___
53 Transcript listings
56 Fire's start
60 Boeing plane
64 Teheran resident
65 Christie's "Death on the ___"
66 Mining locale
67 Trousers
68 Sporty 60's cars
69 Kids' winter schoolday wish

DOWN

1 Newts in transition
2 Trumpet sound
3 Genesis garden
4 Avis offering
5 "Once in Love With ___"
6 Parlor seat
7 David Mamet's "Speed-the-___"
8 Jeb of Bull Run fame
9 Essences
10 Not balanced
11 VH1 rival
12 Before, once
13 Skedaddled
18 Road crew's supply
19 Spanish streams
23 Lively old dance
25 Epic film screenful
26 Temptresses
27 Do 60's clothing designs
28 Snare parts
29 Mr. Hemingway
30 Think creatively
32 "___ bin ein Berliner"
33 Was aware of
36 "___ the season . . ."
37 Letters after Daniel Moynihan's name
39 Newly formed
40 Witch
41 Applications
46 Diagonal
47 Totaling
48 Kicks out
50 Birdlife
52 W.W. II agcy.
54 Passage out
55 Breakthrough battle in Normandy
57 Stratford's stream
58 Completely fix
59 Was in the loop
60 Not guzzle
61 Pitcher's stat
62 Vehicle with sliding doors
63 "You betcha!"

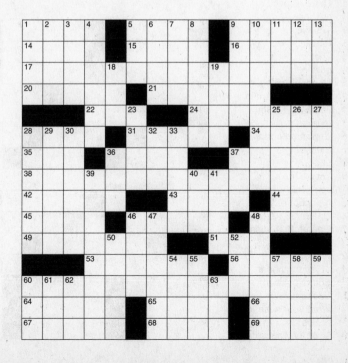

52

by Peter Gordon

ACROSS

1 Wings
5 Rick's love in "Casablanca"
9 Carry's partner
13 One of 39-Across
14 On toast, in diner slang
15 Commedia dell' ___
16 Intended
17 Illuminated sign
18 MTV's "The ___ World"
19 One of 39-Across
21 One of 39-Across
23 Shoebox marking
24 Sex researcher Hite
25 "Welcome" site
28 Europe's highest active volcano
30 Took care of
34 Labor Dept. division
36 Troubles
38 Practice piece
39 Theme of this puzzle
42 Monopoly piece
43 Jazz singer James
44 Jonathan Larson musical
45 Unwanted noise
47 Simplicity
49 Lao-___
50 Tackle box contents
52 Neighbor of Wyo.
54 One of 39-Across
57 One of 39-Across
61 Part of 36-24-36
62 Whitish
64 Ab strengthener
65 Bridge position
66 Uniform
67 What your nose knows
68 Lover of Aphrodite
69 Actress Russo
70 Info

DOWN

1 One of the Baldwins
2 Rachel's sister, in the Bible
3 "Bull Durham" character
4 Main course
5 Brainstorm
6 Bagel topper
7 Sound of a basket
8 Part of a pregame ceremony
9 One of 39-Across
10 Calculus calculation
11 Symbol on a Cowboy's helmet
12 Remained fast
13 Baseball V.I.P.'s
20 Fix a road
22 Some native New Yorkers
24 Greets the general
25 Naphthalene repels them
26 "___ in the Dark"
27 Angle symbol
29 "Good going!"
31 Comforter
32 Perfect places
33 Al ___
35 February stones
37 Mlle., in Spain
40 Untouchable Ness
41 Mr. Arafat
46 One of 39-Across
48 Town in central New Jersey
51 Jack
53 Casual comment
54 It erupted on October 27, 1986
55 When repeated, a 1997 Jim Carrey comedy
56 Church part
57 Kind of pool
58 Put away
59 Not theirs
60 Brit. legislators
63 Novelist Deighton

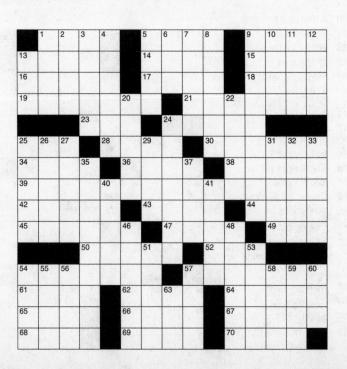

ACROSS

1 Castle protection
5 Watch chains
9 Moby-Dick, for one
14 Tuneful Fitzgerald
15 Nabisco cookie
16 Sponsorship
17 Coal stratum
18 True
19 Affixes in a scrapbook, say
20 Willie Mays at the Y?
23 Traffic arteries
24 Corrida cry
25 Olympic awards
28 Study of verse
32 Standing
33 Horse color
35 Slice
36 Crossword by Joe DiMaggio, e.g.?
40 Somme summer
41 TV's Nick at ___
42 NBC newsman Roger
43 She played the pretty woman in "Pretty Woman"
46 Not mono
47 Former Mideast inits.
48 Was inquisitive
50 Ken Griffey Jr. at 100?
56 Disappearing phone features
57 Final notice
58 Part of a marching band
59 Wally's pal in "Leave It to Beaver"
60 Post-Christmas event
61 Dutch cheese
62 Hippie attire
63 Ogles
64 Lairs

DOWN

1 Phoenix suburb
2 Designer Cassini
3 Jai ___
4 American larch
5 Former Supreme Court Justice Abe
6 Mountain nymph
7 Rays
8 Alone
9 Move rapidly from side to side
10 Footballer's protection
11 Chills
12 Legal claim
13 Test-track curve
21 Nick of "The Prince of Tides"
22 Opposite of everybody
25 Notorious Lansky
26 Muse with a lyre
27 Star in Cygnus
28 Leaf
29 Less welcoming
30 ___ pie (sweetheart)
31 French pen
33 Reformer Jacob
34 It's west of Que.
37 ___ nous (confidentially)
38 Citer
39 Like a first draft
44 Geometer of 300 B.C.
45 Workers' rewards
46 Ice hockey equipment
48 Cornered
49 Photog's request
50 Helper
51 Zippo
52 Sniffer
53 Classic art subject
54 Israel's Abba
55 Butts
56 Society girl

54

by Ed Early

ACROSS

1 Pile
5 Alternative to plastic at a supermarket
10 Winter transport
14 Stewpot
15 Where Sun Valley is
16 Fashioned
17 Crockett or Jones
18 Static
19 Mideast bigwig
20 Lose it
21 Vessel in an alcove
22 Society's 400
23 It's a waste of time
27 Thespian
30 Lily plants
31 Vehicles with booms
33 Bread for a stew, e.g.
34 Missile berth
38 Inner city structure
41 Some sheep
42 Terhune title character
43 Cram into the hold
44 Warner Brothers' ___ J. Fudd
46 Antique shop item
47 1967 Agatha Christie thriller
52 Jeopardy
53 Nicotine's partner
54 Inventor Elias
58 Chapters in world history
59 Well-coordinated
61 Privy to
62 Malicious
63 Butter up?
64 Hardly Mr. Cool
65 New Year's Eve song word

66 Hold for later, as big news
67 Legs, to a zoot suiter

DOWN

1 Bricklayers carry them
2 Flair
3 Thomas ___ Edison
4 Corner conveniences
5 Betty Grable's photo, for one
6 Idolizes
7 Modern driller?
8 Remarks requesting elucidation
9 Fish eggs
10 Food fish

11 Female vampire
12 Tweaks a manuscript
13 Rock's ___ and the Dominos
22 Serpentine curve
24 City SSW of Moscow
25 Subjects of clashes
26 Second-year students, for short
27 Yearn
28 Brag
29 Domesticated
32 Convinces of
34 Nero Wolfe's activity
35 Roman road
36 ___ Strauss & Co.
37 Hydrox rival

39 Menaces for warplanes
40 Inscribe for good
44 Slippery one
45 Commercial center in Venice
47 Olympians' blades
48 Having chutzpah
49 Bathtub part
50 Knit goods thread
51 In leaf
55 Draft classification
56 Apple spoiler
57 Winds up
59 Stomach muscles, for short
60 Toujours ___

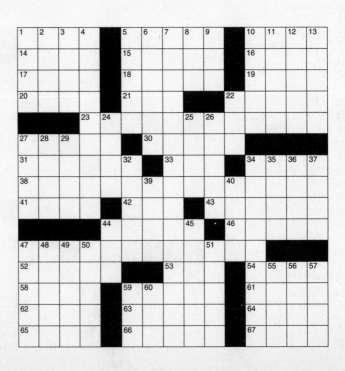

by Peter Gordon

55

ACROSS

1 Step
6 Canyon reply
10 Place to plop down
14 Vietnam's capital
15 Sticky stuff
16 Building additions
17 Mimicking
18 Fraternity rush period
20 French article
21 Pulitzer winner James
23 Kitchen appliances
24 Took out to dinner
26 Trophy display room
27 Young 'un
28 Note excusing tardiness
33 Access AOL, e.g.
36 "___ Misbehavin' "
37 "Blondie" kid
38 Rocky's nickname, with "the"
41 Gangster's girl
42 What unfriendly dogs do
43 Mournful poem
44 Simple folk
46 Have a debt
47 Mauna ___
48 Joining
52 More convenient
56 Ever's partner
57 Neither's partner
58 Brand of cocoa
60 With 61-Down, a California city
62 Bridge-crossing fee
63 Pain in the neck?
64 They bend in prayer
65 Sunburn soother
66 Lascivious look
67 Football gains

DOWN

1 Commandment word
2 Become narrow
3 Licorice flavor
4 Charged atom
5 Tubular pasta
6 Urged (on)
7 Apple leftover
8 Farmer's tool
9 Light musical work
10 Stitched
11 Designer Cassini
12 Run away
13 Questions
19 "Citizen ___"
22 Understand
25 Many of the Marshall Islands
26 "The Divine Comedy" writer
28 Shopping aids
29 Blowgun ammunition
30 "I cannot tell ___"
31 Visibility reducer
32 Walkman maker
33 Walk falteringly
34 Siouan speaker
35 Big party
36 Activist Bryant
39 Strange
40 1998 name in the news
45 Pub offerings
46 Lennon's mate
48 Racing great Al
49 Word with circle or city
50 Famous
51 What Astroturf replaces
52 "Cómo ___ usted?"
53 M.P.'s quarry
54 Fodder holder
55 ___ of Wight
56 Wimbledon winner, 1975
59 Rocks, to a bartender
61 See 60-Across

56

by Diane C. Baldwin

ACROSS

1 1977 George Burns film
6 Stays idle
10 Sentry's cry
14 Bottom of a suit
15 Blue-pencil
16 Rose's fellow
17 Bad
18 Learning method
19 "___ Lisa"
20 Backs of 45's having a sudden change in direction?
23 "Ah, me!"
24 Moon goddess
25 Operatic soprano Geraldine
28 Gush forth
30 Alfonso XIII's queen
31 Tall footwear for rappers?
36 Bank adjuncts
38 It may be lent
39 Writer Ephron
40 Trackside aid that can't be beat?
45 Buddhism sect
46 Playwright Clifford
47 Certain steak
49 Chatterbox
52 Taj Mahal site
53 Portable writing surface for an equestrian?
57 Inlet
58 Verve
59 Boring fellows
62 Singular fellow
63 Full-fledged
64 Weird
65 Hankerings
66 Skyrocket
67 Dozed

DOWN

1 Harem room
2 Chop
3 Malarkey
4 Eyepiece
5 Old Testament temptress
6 Feudal underlings
7 Hero
8 Former Yugoslav chief
9 Accelerates
10 Burr's duel victim
11 Domicile
12 Kind of cabinet
13 Josh
21 ___-mutuel
22 Albanian foe
25 Exploit
26 Against
27 Highway exit
28 Iranian royalty
29 A sweater uses it
32 Annoyance
33 Seep
34 It's just over 14-Across
35 All there
37 Plugs
41 Like Pindar's works
42 Kitchen gadgets
43 Therefore
44 Diatribes
48 Race (along)
49 Hatfield's foe
50 "Leave me ___!"
51 Starting point in decision making
52 Baseball's Doubleday
54 Hodgepodge
55 One of the Three Bears
56 Serious
60 Lulu
61 Established

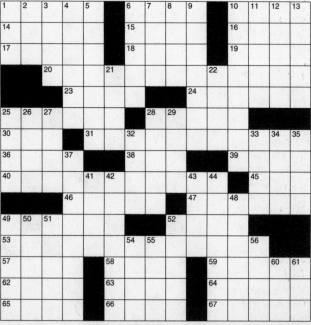

by Nancy Salomon and Bob Frank

ACROSS
1 Like giants
5 Colorado resort
10 Up to the task
14 Inspiration
15 Puppeteer Lewis
16 Emcee Trebek
17 1966 Beatles song
20 Journalist Pyle
21 Door sign during store hours
22 Refusals
23 Newspaper customers
26 Tire pattern
28 Not for minors
30 Begins, as work
33 Classifieds, e.g.
36 Pile
38 Close, as a windbreaker
39 1976 Harry Chapin song
43 Germless
44 Narrate
45 Road-paving stuff
46 New Jersey N.H.L.ers
48 Smacks
51 Poet T. S.___
53 Smacked the baseball good and hard
57 Have title to
59 Hot Springs and others
61 "___ Doone" (1869 novel)
62 1950 Ethel Merman song
66 De-wrinkle
67 Occupied
68 Pottery oven
69 Jamboree shelter
70 Unable to flee
71 Home runs or r.b.i.'s, e.g.

DOWN
1 Princeton or Clemson mascot
2 Love to pieces
3 Hotelier Helmsley
4 "Well, ___!" ("Ain't you somethin'!")
5 Solid ___ rock
6 Like a wallflower
7 El ___, Tex.
8 Blow one's top
9 S.F. footballers, informally
10 "Say ___" (doctor's order)
11 Lane changer's danger
12 Comic Jay
13 Donald and Ivana, Burt and Loni, etc.
18 Monopoly acquisition
19 Reason to say "Gesundheit!"
24 German industrial locale
25 Got some shuteye
27 Working hard
29 "The Canterbury ___"
31 Big brass instrument
32 O, on a telephone: Abbr.
33 Multiple choice choices
34 Strike out, as text
35 Eisenhower opponent
37 Becomes tiresome
40 Follow closely
41 Join the military
42 Bear's scratcher
47 Actress Loren
49 ___ Alto, Calif.
50 Baby deliverers, in birth announcements
52 Corrupt
54 Mom's urging to a picky eater
55 ___ Gay (W.W. II plane)
56 Intimidate
57 Parting words?
58 "The Way We ___"
60 Elitist's rejection
63 Big bang maker
64 Govt. property overseer
65 Whimsical

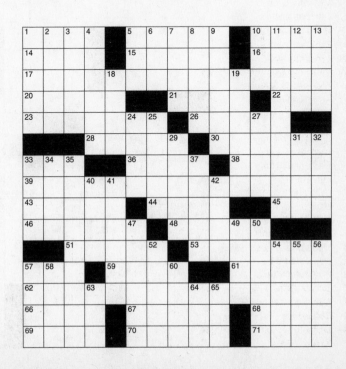

58

by Arthur S. Verdesca

ACROSS

1 Carried on
6 "Think Fast, Mr. ___" (1937 mystery)
10 Dour
14 Single-handedly
15 ". . . and make it snappy!"
16 Field of work
17 Poles, e.g.
18 Fingerprint or dropped handkerchief, say
19 Kimono sashes
20 Oppose
23 Some ancient writings
25 Exploit
26 Just-passing grade
27 Gone by
28 Mournful cries
31 Drudges
33 Dinner at boot camp
35 The Baltic, e.g.
36 Home on the farm
37 Wall Street fixture
42 Exclamations of regret
43 Bud's pal
44 Empty, in math
46 "Amerika" author
49 Film critic Jeffrey
51 The Greatest
52 Lofty lyric
53 Utter
55 Asian capital
57 Like some tenors
61 Mean one
62 Compote fruit
63 Fine suit material
66 Property claim
67 Island dance
68 Bequeath
69 Lavish affection (on)
70 Site of Iowa State
71 Bud Grace comic strip

DOWN

1 Is no longer
2 "Is that ___?"
3 Kicker's target
4 Accredited diplomat
5 Catch sight of
6 Jet speed measure
7 Capital near the 60th parallel
8 Ford debut of 1986
9 Makes the first bid
10 Gentle firelight
11 Psychic energy, to Freud
12 Married
13 Interlocks
21 Newsstands
22 Nasal partitions
23 Tennis's Shriver
24 Census data
29 Teeny
30 Without strict oversight
32 Boston suburb
34 Overcharge, slangily
36 Railroad switches
38 Many a climactic movie scene
39 Dove's cry
40 Protector
41 Raines of 40's–50's film
45 Author ___ Yutang
46 German goblin
47 Slow ballet dance
48 Animal that drives rabbits from their burrows
49 Lecture hall
50 Not demand everything one wants
54 Beginning
56 Tree cutter
58 Actor Auberjonois
59 Sound in body
60 Times to live through
64 56, to Flavius
65 Grant's opposite

ACROSS

1 Labor's partner, in a garage bill
6 Pro ___ (proportionate)
10 Some urban air
14 Big name at video arcades
15 Dutch cheese
16 No-no: Var.
17 Homeowners may take them out
20 Uttered
21 Corn units
22 Watermelon part
23 Tee precursor
24 Author Tyler
25 Found at this place
27 Good-as-new tire
29 Put down, slangily
30 Caribbean, e.g.
31 Op ___
32 Elsie's chew
33 Bank earnings: Abbr.
34 Journalists, as a group
40 "Yo!"
41 Legal thing
42 Org. that gets members reduced motel rates
43 It's found in the ground
44 Exchange I do's
45 All thumbs
49 Made good on, as a loan
51 Jai ___
52 Baked Hawaiian dish
53 Helpful ___
54 Singer Anita
55 Amount to make do with
56 "The Pastoral," formally
59 Big oil company
60 Pastrami place
61 River to the Rhône
62 Glimpsed
63 Historical spans
64 Spanish houses

DOWN

1 Overtaker on the road
2 "Relax, soldiers!"
3 Bigot
4 Walked (on)
5 Confession in a confessional
6 Send back to a lower court
7 Like a lot
8 Sailors
9 Tsp. or tbs.
10 One step
11 Milk of ___
12 Following orders
13 Gloomy guy
18 Like alcohol that's unfit for drinking
19 Some college tests, for short
24 Prefix with dynamic
25 Treehouses and such
26 Basketball's Archibald
28 W.W. II fliers: Abbr.
29 Comment made while slapping the forehead
32 Pennies: Abbr.
34 Comic book superhero
35 Open receiver's cry, maybe
36 Lens
37 Sunburned
38 H. H. Munro's pen name
39 Playing marble
44 "Get ___ it!"
45 Singer Morissette
46 Peaks
47 Spots for speakers
48 Spode pieces
50 Susan of "Goldengirl"
51 Writer ___ Rogers St. Johns
54 Dispatcher's word
55 "Mona ___"
56 Undergrad degrees
57 Poem of praise
58 [their mistake, not mine]

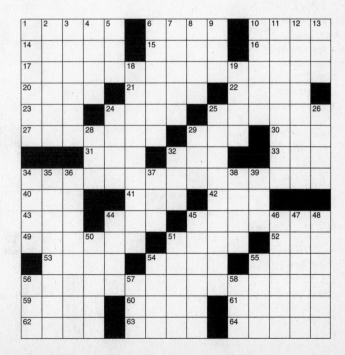

60

by Jeremy Thomas Paine

ACROSS

1 Some fathers: Abbr.
4 Winter Palace ruler
8 Big name in hotels
14 Private eye, for short
15 $75/night, e.g.
16 Microscopic creature
17 Like: Suffix
18 Picnic raiders
19 Maritime hazard in W. W. II
20 Richard Benjamin's film debut, 1969
23 Stubborn beasts
24 Hospital cry
25 Enzyme ending
26 ___-Israeli relations
27 Dangerous date for Caesar
28 Ripening agent
29 Vamoosed
31 E.M.T.'s procedure
33 & 34 1996 action film sequel
37 "Rubber Soul," "Revolver" and others
38 Only so far
40 Apple or pear
43 Disavow
44 "Leave ___ Beaver"
45 Article in Arles
46 Quake locale
48 Tempestuous spirit?
49 Cage/Shue picture of 1995

52 Clapboards, e.g.
53 Locale
54 Inits. in long distance
55 Beloved of Aphrodite
56 ___ about (approximately)
57 New: Prefix
58 Least cooked
59 Politician Gingrich
60 "Don't give up!"

DOWN

1 Marks of shame
2 Backup help
3 Academic types
4 Shore dinner entree
5 Off-the-wall
6 One who shows up

7 Saved
8 Carries
9 Permeate
10 Weaver's apparatus
11 It may land in hot water
12 Hardly brainy
13 Sadat's predecessor
21 Disastrous collapse
22 Surg. areas
27 Little devils
28 Large wardrobe
30 Navigator's need
31 Supercomputer name
32 Bad sound for a balloonist
34 Actress Joan of "Rebecca"

35 Plaintiff or defendant
36 Aardvark
38 Runs to mom about
39 "Anna Karenina" author
40 Astronomical object
41 Iroquoian tribe
42 Field
43 Grooved on
46 The end
47 Dread
48 Turn aside
50 Morning glory, e.g.
51 Put away

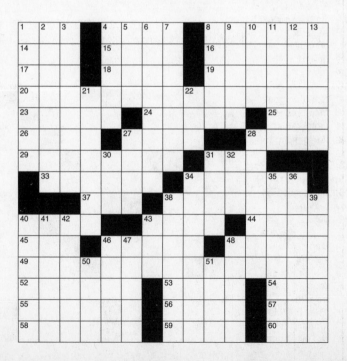

by Cynthia Joy Higgins 61

ACROSS

1 Number on a baseball card
5 Beginning with frost
10 Like most nursery rhymes: Abbr.
14 Twosome
15 To have, in Paris
16 Timber wolf
17 Wheel rotator
18 Butcher's ship?
20 Squander
22 "To your health!," e.g.
23 A fisherman may spin one
24 Museum V.I.P.
26 Postal worker's ship?
30 Gulf Coast bird
31 Yemeni port
32 Second addendum to a letter: Abbr.
35 Most people born in August
36 Spoke wildly
38 Codger
39 Pins or penny preceder
40 Fillet of ___
41 Beta's follower
42 Manicurist's ship?
45 Summer park event
49 Boaters pull them
50 Informed (of)
51 Storm protectors
55 Highlighter's ship?
58 Pass over
59 Espies
60 Become accustomed (to)
61 Egypt's main water supply
62 Misses the mark
63 Tower of ___
64 Grades 1–6: Abbr.

DOWN

1 Meat in a can
2 Curbside call
3 Is under the weather
4 Railroad bridges
5 Actress Anderson of "Baywatch"
6 Closer to 50–50
7 Turnpike
8 Prestigious sch. near Boston
9 Rainbow
10 Choir voices
11 Skipping, as an event
12 Portly and then some
13 Sur's opposite, in México
19 Sometimes illegal auto maneuver
21 Treaty
24 Beach washer
25 Critic Rex
26 Sandwich that's been heated
27 "A Death in the Family" author
28 Multivitamin supplement
29 Get tangled
32 Magnificence
33 Fleshy fruit
34 Polaris, e.g.
36 Crowd sound
37 Came down
38 Crowning event
40 Show scorn
41 Braced
43 Stick (to)
44 Victory emblem
45 ___ célèbre
46 Tenant's counterpart
47 Consumerist Ralph
48 Green garnish
51 Rebuff
52 Olympic track champion Zatopek
53 Tick off
54 Flower holder
56 Conservative's foe: Abbr.
57 ___ heartbeat (instantly)

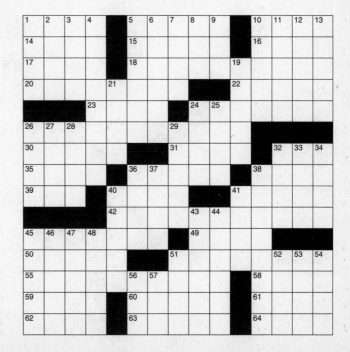

62

by Stephanie Spadaccini

ACROSS
1 Skiing mecca
5 Dogs and cats, e.g.
9 Hidden room's secret opening
14 Comic Sahl
15 "Dies ___"
16 Idolize
17 Vulgarian
18 Seagoing: Abbr.
19 Have a feeling about
20 X
23 Old-time entertainer ___ Tucker
24 Morse code component
25 Quiche, e.g.
26 The Emerald Isle
28 Hairpiece
31 60's protest
34 "Time ___ My Side" (Rolling Stones hit)
35 Demonstrate
36 X
39 Music synthesizer
40 Malarial fever
41 The Phantom's instrument
42 Switch positions
43 Quaker's "you"
44 Prefix with nuptial
45 ___ Paulo, Brazil
46 Italian cheese
49 X
54 Slow mover
55 ___ Orange, N.J.
56 Hollow response
57 Pancake syrup flavor
58 Friend, to Françoise
59 Actress Perlman
60 Like some stomachs
61 Look closely
62 Burn quickly

DOWN
1 Prefix with dexterity
2 Makes off with illegally
3 TV teaser
4 Big and strong
5 Finger that curls
6 Rub out
7 Tight as a drum
8 Clockmaker Thomas
9 Die, euphemistically
10 Highly skilled
11 Forbidden thing
12 Once, once
13 Attorney F. ___ Bailey
21 Zoo beast
22 Patsy's pal on "Absolutely Fabulous"
26 In the style of: Suffix
27 Debaucher
28 Supporter of the American Revolution
29 Little bit
30 17th-century actress Nell
31 Japanese wrestling
32 Get ___ the ground floor
33 W.B.A. calls
34 "Come Back, Little Sheba" playwright
35 Naked runners
37 "Yippee!"
38 Designer Kamali
43 Writing pad
44 Baggage handler
45 "Look happy!"
46 First name in TV talk
47 Hiding spot
48 Milo or Tessie
49 Ginger cookie
50 Blabs
51 Spring
52 Renown
53 Fly like an eagle
54 Texas Mustangs, for short

by Elizabeth C. Gorski

ACROSS

1 Fearless
5 Nicholas I or II
9 Sears rival
14 The Buckeye State
15 Queen of Olympus
16 1960's enemy capital
17 "___ Like It Hot"
18 Completely bollix
19 Positive pole
20 "Bleak House" writer
23 C.I.A. predecessor
24 Lend a hand
25 Stick on
29 More than once around the track
31 J.F.K.'s predecessor
34 "Cheesy" Italian city
35 Germany's ___ Valley
36 Not written
37 Storyteller's embellishment
40 Win's opposite
41 Silly syllables
42 Hopping mad
43 "Aye, aye!"
44 Give up
45 Gets around
46 Halloween greeting
47 151 on a monument
48 Young ones
56 Use, as a chaise longue
57 Author Haley
58 Inventive thought
59 "Remember the ___"
60 ___-mutuel (form of betting)
61 Shooting matches?
62 Razor sharpener
63 Pitcher
64 Reply to "Are you hurt?"

DOWN

1 49-Down variety
2 Cry of anticipation
3 Peru's capital
4 Not the retiring type
5 Beat hard
6 Children's Dr.
7 Mojave-like
8 Punjabi princess
9 Military uniform
10 Like a horse or lion
11 Soon, to a poet
12 Serling and Stewart
13 Gift from Monica to Bill
21 Nearby
22 Bay of Naples isle
25 With suitability
26 Nevada skiing locale
27 Rapunzel feature
28 Rock concert necessities
29 Wood-shaping tool
30 Sounds of delight
31 Great fear
32 "The Divine Comedy" poet
33 Nobody ___ business
35 Breeder
36 Gumbo ingredient
38 Classic theater
39 Kind of duty
44 Like arcade games
45 Magical drink
46 Stomach soother
47 Dear, in Dijon
48 Delta deposit
49 Fall fruit
50 Stare
51 Cat's scratcher
52 Green fruit
53 Mild cheese
54 In legend, he fiddled in a fire
55 Neighbor of Alta.
56 ___ Vegas

64

by Frances Hansen

ACROSS

1 Polish border river
5 Lazy girl?
10 It's uplifting
13 Comic's missiles
14 Strangle
15 Stimpy's TV pal
16 Character created by 58-Across
18 F.D.R. measure
19 Spiral-horned sheep
20 "Ready, ___ . . . !"
21 Tiny stream
22 Employers of 58-Across
25 Greek H
26 Army cops
27 Frozen desserts
28 German spa
30 Claiborne or Smith
32 West Pointer
33 1951 film featuring 58-Across
37 Patrick of "Marat/Sade"
40 Ernie Els's org.
41 Comic DeLuise
44 Patti of opera lore
47 Under the weather
49 Caviar
51 Where 58-Across died, 1979
54 Bandy words
55 Burgle
56 Parrots, in a way
57 SST's fly over it: Abbr.
58 Memorable Big Top star born 12/9/1898
60 King of Kings
61 Drops in the letter box
62 Ciardi's "___ a Man"
63 Leandro's love
64 "I give up!"
65 So-called monster's home

DOWN

1 Surgeon's decision
2 You're working on one
3 Showed on TV again
4 Sanctuary
5 ___-fi
6 Old Polish lancer
7 Pyramid and cube
8 Like some arms
9 Society page word
10 Grilled
11 Satiated
12 Wall Street worker
16 ". . . gimble in the ___": Carroll
17 Nun's headdress
21 Decorative strip of fabric
23 "Oh, you wish!"
24 Medieval chest
29 Of a stone pillar
31 Nuke
34 "Who does he think ___!"
35 End-of-week cry
36 Xylophone tool
37 Knead
38 Converting device: Var.
39 First name in TV talk
42 Gregg Olson and others
43 Early assembly-line cars
45 Bates of "Psycho"
46 Extremely tiny
48 Commit unalterably
50 "Duck soup"
52 Clear as ___
53 Part of a sentence, in linguistics
58 Cassowary's cousin
59 Mao ___-tung

ACROSS

1 A three-of-a-kind beats it
5 Glided
9 Stun
14 Too
15 Newsweek rival
16 Poorer, as excuses go
17 Formal dance
18 Give off
19 Trim limbs
20 Something of trivial importance
23 "My Cousin Vinny" Oscar winner Marisa
24 Televise
25 Bad __ (German spa)
28 Alcott classic
33 Spawning fish
37 Buck's mate
38 Michelangelo statue
39 Achingly desire
41 "The Mary Tyler Moore Show" co-star
43 Make amends
44 Muhammad __
45 To be, in Toulouse
46 Don Ho's theme song
50 Porker's pad
51 Actress Zadora
52 "The Lion King" lion
57 Windmill setting
62 Think out loud
64 __-American relations
65 Inter __
66 String bean's opposite
67 Oklahoma city
68 Huge
69 Test, as a garment
70 Certain NCO's
71 Gaelic

DOWN

1 Big name in brewing
2 "Remember the __"
3 44-Across's faith
4 Esther of TV's "Good Times"
5 Part of a process
6 Prom night transport
7 Ape
8 Particular
9 Brand for Bowser
10 Stallion's mate
11 Kind of park
12 Buddhist state
13 Before, in poetry
21 Diamond __
22 Three, in Torino
26 Poet's constraint
27 Entrap
29 Bride's words
30 High craggy hill
31 Depression-era program: Abbr.
32 River to the Seine
33 Tiffs
34 Bandleader's cry
35 Fame's opposite
36 When said three times, a liar's policy
40 Jan. follower
41 Pipe bend
42 Go out, as a flame
44 Letting up
47 Wire service inits.
48 Slants
49 Opposite NNW
53 "__ at the office"
54 Back tooth
55 Ecstasy
56 __ worse than death
58 Not __ many words
59 Sign gas
60 Measuring standard
61 Axles
62 Many a time
63 Golfer's goal

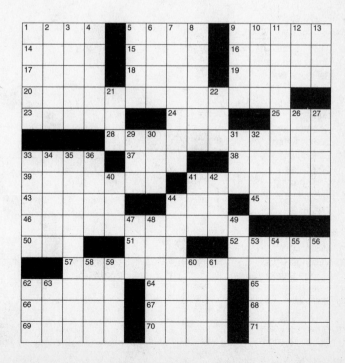

66

by Patrick Jordan

ACROSS

1 Garden crasher
5 Gather up
10 Mary ___ cosmetics
13 Less inept
15 Futuristic slave
16 "___ Gotta Be Me"
17 Addition to the family
19 Replayed tennis shot
20 Recent hires
21 New Zealand tribesman
23 Hog heaven?
24 Ques. counterpart
25 Rolling Stone Richards
27 Colloquialism for 17-Across
31 Shattered pane piece
34 Individuals
35 "Blame It on ___" (Caine comedy)
36 Game with mallets
37 Religious law
39 "___ never fly!"
40 "Sure thing, skipper!"
41 German car
42 Disconcerted
43 Colloquialism for 17-Across
47 Fool (around)
48 Jerusalem is its cap.
49 Quiz
52 Crockett's last stand
54 Poshness
56 Square dance partner
57 Colloquialism for 17-Across
60 Adam's madam
61 Public persona
62 Ten ___ (long odds)
63 When it's light
64 Behind bars
65 Like many a mistake

DOWN

1 Desires
2 Thumbs up/ thumbs down critic
3 Broncos QB John
4 Figure skater Thomas
5 Marshal Dillon's portrayer
6 Unruly crowds
7 Lawyer's org.
8 Blubber
9 Thwarts
10 Unit of frequency
11 Declare firmly
12 Himalayan legend
14 George's predecessor
18 Russo of "Get Shorty"
22 Versatile transport, for short
25 Bingo relative
26 Utopia
27 Sis's sib
28 Kind of boom
29 Aswan Dam locale
30 Narrated
31 Bickering
32 Boxer Oscar De La ___
33 "Roots" writer
37 Cows' mouthfuls
38 Together, in music
39 Author Fleming
41 Like some exercises
42 Drew a blank
44 ___ Perignon
45 Worked the soil
46 "Gotcha!"
49 Pear variety
50 Teatime treat
51 Tensed, with "up"
52 Not young
53 Volcanic flow
54 Cutting part
55 Get an ___ effort
58 Actress Thurman
59 Broken-down 47-Across

ACROSS

1 Long story
5 Rich kid in "Nancy"
10 Panhandles
14 Shangri-la
15 Hoopster Shaquille
16 One of the Four Corners states
17 Penny purchase, years ago
19 "Ali ___ and the Forty Thieves"
20 "A" or "an"
21 Incomprehensible, as a message
23 Parasite
24 Business bigwig
25 Miss Kett of old comics
28 Liveliness
32 Custard dessert
36 "Horrors!"
38 Rocket stage
39 Gofer
40 Jelly fruit
42 E pluribus ___
43 Throng
45 Seize with a toothpick
46 Forest growth
47 Mortarboard attachment
49 Actress Lanchester
51 Grand jury's activity
53 Pueblo site
58 Jack of "City Slickers"
61 One making a medical inquiry
63 On
64 Penny purchase, years ago
66 Fish entree

67 Treasure store
68 "This round's ___!"
69 Bridge whiz Sharif
70 Gung-ho
71 Poverty

DOWN

1 Flower part
2 Be wild about
3 "Beau ___"
4 Shenanigan
5 Paper towel unit
6 "Going ___, going . . ."
7 Meadow
8 Slow, in music
9 Opposite of youth
10 Penny purchase, years ago
11 Catchall abbr.

12 Kotter of "Welcome Back, Kotter"
13 Certain herring
18 Pain
22 ___ fever (be hot)
24 Endangered Florida creature
26 Dress (up)
27 Therefore
29 Snap-marriage locale
30 Wildebeests
31 Thanksgiving side dish
32 Almanac tidbit
33 Money in Milano
34 Fusses
35 Penny purchase, years ago
37 Model train layout, often

41 Not present: Abbr.
44 Gosh-awful
48 Pinpoint
50 Realtor's unit
52 Quotable catcher Yogi
54 Access the Net
55 Cockamamie
56 ___ fatale
57 No longer a slave
58 El ___, Tex.
59 Elementary particle
60 "Damn Yankees" vamp
61 Cro-Magnon's home
62 Frankfurt's river
65 Machine tooth

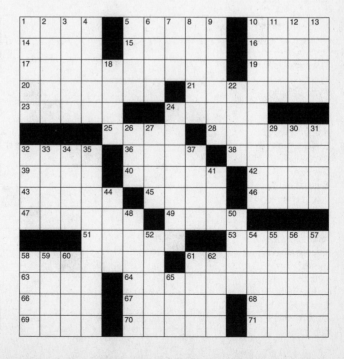

68

by Adam Cohen

ACROSS
1. "In"
5. Faint flicker
10. Hits with a ray gun
14. Author ___ Neale Hurston
15. "Amazing" magician
16. Together, musically
17. Protein components
19. ___ Strip
20. Paraphrased
21. Latter-day Saint
23. Nature goddess
24. Fruit of the Loom competitor
25. Openings
28. Information accessed on a computer
31. Water sources
32. Assumed
33. 1968 hit "Harper Valley ___"
34. Hangover?
35. Roebuck's partner
36. Mimic
37. Ryan's "Love Story" co-star
38. Observe Yom Kippur
39. Speck of land in the sea
40. Deserter
42. Coat of many colors wearer
43. Coeur d'___, Idaho
44. "Stand By Me" singer ___ King
45. Beefed
47. Xylophone-like instruments
51. Singer Falana
52. East African capital
54. Takes advantage of
55. "Good Times" actress Esther
56. Stew ingredient
57. Deli jarful
58. Symbol of freshness
59. Art Deco artist

DOWN
1. Ivan the Terrible, e.g.
2. "Where the heart is"
3. Eye part
4. Biblical hymn
5. Without charge
6. Shoestrings
7. Writer Bagnold
8. Put a wing (on)
9. Slips up, as a dating service
10. Croatian capital
11. It might bob up in conversation
12. "The Godfather" author
13. Penn name
18. Filling stations?
22. "Chestnuts roasting ___ open fire"
24. Le ___, France
25. Take an oath
26. Positive thinking proponent
27. American Dance Theater founder
28. Steak ___
29. Pricey
30. Our planet
32. Crystal rock
35. Run of the mill
36. Come together
38. Pulitzer-winning writer James
39. Ancient part of Asia Minor
41. Rio Grande city
42. It's across the Hudson from New York
44. Jumps (out)
45. Dejected
46. Sub ___ (secretly)
47. 1551, on monuments
48. 1930's heavyweight champ Max
49. Aid in crime
50. Sushi bar drink
53. ___ 180 (turn around, in slang)

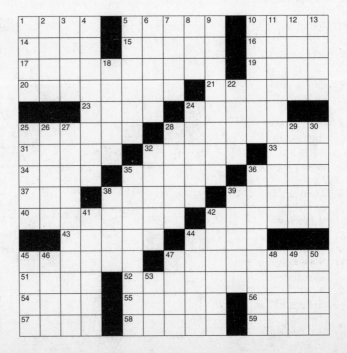

ACROSS

1 Pinkish, as a steak
5 Pitcher's boo-boo
9 Applications
13 Face-to-face exam
14 Annual theater award
15 Leg/foot connector
16 TIM
19 Airline to Stockholm
20 Regarding, in legal memos
21 Ruins a picnic or a Little League game, say
22 Subsidy
23 Challenge
24 Sheriff's star
27 It follows sunset, in poetry
28 "Phooey!"
32 Art photo shade
33 Alpha's opposite
35 A shepherd shepherds it
36 ERIC
39 Honest ___
40 ___ Ababa
41 Make pretty
42 Lipton and Twinings, e.g.
44 Actor Kilmer
45 Hearty steak
46 France's ___ des Saintes
48 ___ chi ch'uan
49 Give a damn?
51 Nuts (over)
52 By way of
55 OK
58 Runs smoothly, as an engine
59 Brownish songbird
60 Start for a kitty
61 "Black Beauty" author Sewell
62 Give for a while
63 Happy or sad feeling

DOWN

1 Steals from
2 Vicinity
3 Lively piano tunes
4 Gin maker Whitney
5 Clyde's partner in crime
6 Eat like ___
7 Queue
8 Fraternity party staple
9 Loose, as shoestrings
10 Body wrapper
11 "Desire Under the ___"
12 Notice
15 At a distance
17 Big honeymoon destination
18 Syracuse's team color
23 Considers
24 Deep-sea explorer William
25 Sleeper's woe
26 Dah's partner
27 90's-style letters
29 Scouting mission, informally
30 In the know
31 Where Memphis is: Abbr.
32 Improvise, musically
33 ___ Methuselah
34 The Black Stallion, e.g.
37 Adjective modifier
38 Bride's declaration
43 ___ Madres
45 Remnant
47 Puts (down)
48 Spoken for
49 Flabbergast
50 Frayed
51 Pierce with a tusk
52 Chianti, e.g.
53 Division word
54 Elderly
55 Health resort
56 Mouse catcher
57 Hydroelectric project

by Susan Harrington Smith

ACROSS

1 Shells, for short
5 "Not on ___!"
9 Mark left by Zorro?
13 Instrument for an étude
15 Pre-stereo
16 Dramatic entrance announcement
17 Blooper
18 Verve
19 Hertz rival
20 Little guy getting the third degree?
23 Wee, to Burns
25 "Gosh!"
26 Kind of crew
27 Neatly combed curmudgeon?
31 Hunter in the night sky
32 Lamp type
36 Filmmaker Jacques
37 Lesley of "60 Minutes"
39 ___ Penh, Cambodia
41 Ropes, as a dogie
43 Cartoon "Mr."
44 Gambling locale for the taciturn?
47 French dramatist Antonin ___
51 Sounds from Santa
52 Fishing aid
53 Bright-red unglazed china?
57 They may clash in business
58 Shower
59 Addicts
62 Letter for Gandalf
63 Tied
64 Sign up
65 Caddie's bagful

66 Withhold, as funds
67 Concerning

DOWN

1 Mimic
2 Russian space station
3 Tequila drink
4 ___ about (circa)
5 Sauntered
6 Word with crashing or tidal
7 Sir Geraint's wife
8 Like Cinderella's slipper, to her stepsisters
9 Jump involuntarily
10 Quibble
11 ". . . can you spare ___?"
12 Grating
14 Beginning

21 Jeans brand
22 Tramp
23 Robert Burns, for one
24 Subway artwork
28 Louis-Philippe and others
29 Gulf
30 "Yay, team!"
33 3.7 and 4.0, e.g.
34 Train V.I.P.'s
35 Nary a soul
37 Fused
38 4:00 gathering
40 No longer worth discussing
42 Hare's tail
43 Poe's "The ___ of the Red Death"
45 Climb, in a way
46 Fortune 500 listings: Abbr.

47 On the qui vive
48 Scamp
49 Dinner leftover for Bowser
50 Donkeys
54 Carry on
55 "Très ___!"
56 Annapolis sch.
60 Twaddle
61 ___-pitch softball

by Gregory E. Paul

ACROSS

1 Thumb-twiddling
5 Leapfrogs
10 ___ Bator, Mongolia
14 Make airtight
15 ___ a time (singly)
16 "Cleopatra" backdrop
17 "Yes!"
19 Darling
20 Sendak's "Where the Wild Things ___"
21 Composer Satie
22 Soviet leader Brezhnev
24 Semiautomatic rifle
26 Land of the llama
27 Red-white-and-blue inits.
28 Information bank
32 Passing notice?
35 King of the jungle
37 What a lumberjack leaves behind
38 River to the Rio Grande
40 SSW's opposite
41 Like a haunted house
42 Skyward
43 Persian ___
45 Person to go out with
46 Round Table knight
48 C.I.O.'s partner
50 Skip
51 "Don't move!"
55 Snake-haired woman of myth
58 35-Across's sound
59 ___ de France
60 Walkie-talkie word
61 "Yes!"
64 Needles' partner
65 Train making all stops
66 Med school subj.
67 Otherwise
68 Manicurist's board
69 Optimistic

DOWN

1 Writer Asimov
2 Actress Winger
3 Tattoo remover
4 "Xanadu" rock grp.
5 Diary
6 Loosen, as a knot
7 Overly docile
8 Chum
9 Sharp-pointed instrument
10 "Yes!"
11 Mortgage
12 Jai ___
13 Uncool one
18 Arrival gifts in Honolulu
23 Remove, as marks
25 "Yes!"
26 See 51-Down
28 Coffee break snack
29 Glow
30 Slugged, old-style
31 Sportsman's blade
32 October's birthstone
33 Composer Bartók
34 PC picture
36 Fort Knox unit
39 Cherries' leftovers
44 So as to cause death
47 Apt
49 Raise crops
51 With 26-Down, a rooftop energy device
52 Elton John's instrument
53 Arm bones
54 Not handling criticism well
55 Brood
56 Like Darth Vader
57 Cub Scout groups
58 Derby
62 ___ Kippur
63 Something to lend or bend

72

by Lyell Rodieck

ACROSS

1 Auntie, dramatically
5 "La Classe de danse" artist
10 Birds in barns
14 Quizmaster Trebek
15 Humble
16 Cookie since 1912
17 Asset for 34-Across?
20 Bee activity
21 Classical lyric poet
22 Creative work
23 Book after Nehemiah: Abbr.
24 Sites of crosses
27 Meadow sounds
28 ___ Na Na
31 No longer on the plate
32 Doughnut shapes
33 Extent
34 Circus act
37 Place for a revival
38 Kind of desk
39 Flowerless plants
40 Before, in poetry
41 Rules out
42 Not yet sunk
43 Common hello or goodbye
44 Habeas corpus, for one
45 Spicy cuisine
48 Takes advance orders for
52 Liability for 34-Across?
54 The Urals are west of it
55 Dinner bird
56 Witty Bombeck
57 Put salt on, maybe
58 Bridge positions
59 Time of decision

DOWN

1 Handy computers
2 "There oughta be ___!"
3 Southwest sight
4 Glad-handing type
5 Father of Xerxes
6 Dark shades
7 Thieves' group
8 Numbskull
9 Leaves the dock
10 Zing
11 Saran, e.g.
12 Preyer
13 London or New York district
18 Be about to happen
19 Feedbag feed
23 Jumping the gun
24 Romantic adventure
25 More cold and wet
26 Agreeing (with)
27 Marina sights
28 Veep Agnew
29 ___-Barbera (big name in cartoons)
30 Feeling of apprehension
32 Coil
33 Took the heat badly
35 Search like wolves
36 Aloof
41 Island near Java
42 Rugged ridges
43 Actor Tom of "The Dukes of Hazzard"
44 Extract by force
45 Symbol of noncommunication
46 Trick
47 Oscar winner Jannings
48 Light: Prefix
49 Byron or Tennyson
50 Tibetan monk
51 Corset part
53 ___ fault (overly so)

ACROSS

1 Begin, as school
6 St. Peter's Square figure
10 Broadway "Auntie"
14 Peter of "Casablanca"
15 Cards up one's sleeve?
16 Muslim holy man
17 Any one of God's creatures
18 Classic Bette Davis line from "Beyond the Forest"
20 Second-place finishers
22 Call forth
23 WNW's opposite
24 DiCaprio, to fans
25 Lock opener
26 Proceeding easily, at last
31 Dallas's locale
32 Metal to be refined
33 Res ___ loquitur
37 Tempers
38 Flogged
40 Underground vegetable
41 Miss America wears one
42 ___ de Janeiro
43 Word on mail from Spain
44 Oscar-winning role for Tom Hanks
47 Greyhound, e.g.
50 Slalom curve
51 It's perpendicular to long.
52 Golden Delicious and others
54 1966 Simon and Garfunkel hit
59 High school parking lot fixture
61 Religious law
62 Soho socials
63 Responsibility
64 Blackjack phrase
65 Flubs
66 Sage
67 Run off to the chapel

DOWN

1 Exile site for Napoleon
2 Christmas
3 Speaker of Cooperstown
4 Cube inventor Rubik
5 Brief turndown to an invitation
6 Oklahoma Indian
7 Newspaperman Adolph
8 Stew morsel
9 Highly regarded
10 Skirt style
11 Frenzied: Var.
12 Mrs. Eisenhower
13 Running on ___
19 Not straight
21 Fire remnant
24 Tackle box item
26 Mayberry jail habitué
27 Actress Miles
28 Alimony receivers
29 Poison ivy woe
30 Courtroom addressee, with "your"
33 "___ to differ!"
34 Lima's land
35 Appear
36 Surmounting
38 Medieval weapon
39 Broadcasts
43 Diplomat's aide
44 Corn, to chickens
45 Run out
46 Uncle ___
47 Sew with loose stitches
48 Certain berth
49 Weapon that's thrown
53 More or ___
54 Radio man Don
55 Train track
56 Word after catch or hang
57 Free ticket
58 Bouncing baby's seat
60 Single: Prefix

74

by Nancy Salomon

ACROSS

1 Nabisco cracker
5 Respond to seeing red?
9 Central highway
14 Brainstorm
15 Not taped
16 Former
17 Summon Warsaw citizens?
19 Hint of color
20 Opposite of masc.
21 F.B.I. workers
23 The I's have them
24 Mileage testing grp.
25 Undercover operation
27 Small change for a Brit
32 Unimagined
35 Broadcast studio sign
36 Any hit by Elvis
38 Hubbub
39 Artificial locks
40 Summon the elected?
42 Hit on the knuckles
43 Sorbonne summer
44 Bottle capacity
45 Common nest locale
47 Fine point
49 Under pressure
51 ___ Nile
53 Opponent of D.D.E.
54 Songstress Vikki
56 Dressed, so to speak
59 Trendy
62 Talk a blue streak
64 Summon actress Sharon?

66 ___ football (indoor sport)
67 Cartoonist Peter
68 "A Clockwork Orange" hooligan
69 Cattail's locale
70 Made a bubble, in a way
71 Crème de la crème

DOWN

1 Jazz phrase
2 Goofing off
3 Broncos or Chargers
4 Veer suddenly
5 Campaign ad feature
6 Scrabble piece
7 Broiling locale
8 Pains in the neck

9 To the point
10 The East
11 Summon Michael Jordan and John Stockton?
12 Take-out words
13 War god
18 Office fastener
22 Gravy spot
24 Prefix with center
26 Glaciers
27 Like illegally parked cars, sometimes
28 Get together
29 Summon a cable magnate?
30 Derby prospect
31 French fashion magazines
33 "Waste not, want not," e.g.

34 Ran
37 Malicious gossip
41 Was bedbound
46 Snaky letter
48 Chefs' wear
50 Was almost out of inventory
52 Get-well site
54 Study late
55 Ambiance
57 Baseball's Yastrzemski
58 German article
59 Links target
60 Washington bills
61 Student's book
63 "No dice"
65 Bill

ACROSS

1 Playwright William
5 Some Pennsylvania Dutch
10 Carol
14 That, in France
15 Division of a long poem
16 Hard rain?
17 Best Picture of 1995
19 Tex. neighbor
20 Car that was always black
21 Catch red-handed
22 Swerve
23 Arctic bird
25 Goalie's job
27 Bed turner?
31 ___ and anon
32 "I didn't know that!"
33 Appliquéd
38 Enticed
40 Crow's cry
42 Barber's work
43 ___ of Capricorn
45 Brit. fliers
47 Roman road
48 "Cracklin' Rosie" singer
51 "Shane," e.g.
55 "Last one ___ a rotten egg!"
56 Robust
57 Much of 35-Down's terr.
59 Melodious
63 With defects and all
64 Group that makes contracts
66 Fasting time
67 Drive away
68 "The African Queen" screenwriter James
69 Organization with a lodge
70 One of the Astaires
71 Slothful

DOWN

1 Part of a nuclear arsenal, for short
2 Fiddling emperor
3 Pleased
4 Listen in (on)
5 German warning
6 Fannie ___
7 ___ instant (quickly)
8 Italian road
9 Centers of activity
10 Push
11 Like some old buckets
12 Frasier's brother on "Frasier"
13 Harsh reflection
18 Actress Sommer
24 "Hold on ___!"
26 Payments to doctors
27 Moola
28 Assert
29 Fix up
30 Oyster's center
34 Capricious
35 Org. formed to contain Communism
36 Bread chamber
37 One who's socially clueless
39 Prime-time hour
41 Desert stream
44 Parts of brains
46 Wangle
49 Accustomed
50 Suffix with million
51 Humpback, e.g.
52 Stand for something
53 Go furtively
54 They may come in a battery
58 Ready to be picked
60 Korbut on the beam
61 Egyptian canal
62 Mind
65 The first of 13: Abbr.

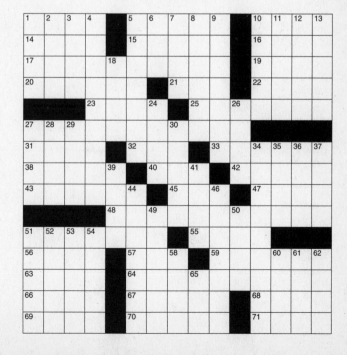

Solving The New York Times Crossword Puzzle Just Got A Little Easier.

Look for these portable-size puzzle books that fit easily into your briefcase, carry-on, or handbag.

Perfect for on the go!

Sit, back, relax and enjoy these easy puzzles.

Never run out of challenges with these brain-bending tough puzzles.

Available at your local bookstore or online at
nytimes.com/nytstore

1

L	O	G	E		A	T	L	A	S		F	O	R	E
A	V	I	D		P	O	I	S	E		A	W	O	L
M	A	G	I		P	A	S	T	E		L	E	E	K
B	L	I	T	H	E	S	P	I	R	I	T		
		O	A	T			R	E	H	A	B		
R	E	C	A	L	L		L	I	B	E	R	A	T	E
E	M	A	I	L		B	E	S	O		W	O	E	
J	O	L	L	Y	G	R	E	E	N	G	I	A	N	T
E	T	O		A	I	D	E		A	R	I	E	L	
C	E	R	A	M	I	C	S		A	T	T	I	R	E
T	R	Y	S	T			S	R	O					
		H	A	P	P	Y	W	A	R	R	I	O	R	
S	P	E	C		A	R	M	O	R		I	D	L	E
M	E	G	A		C	O	C	O	A		F	E	E	D
U	P	O	N		A	D	A	P	T		T	A	O	S

2

E	L	S	A		A	J	A	R		R	I	L	E	D
D	A	L	I		S	A	N	E		E	V	O	K	E
I	T	E	R		I	N	K	S		L	E	V	E	E
T	H	E	L	M	A	&	L	O	U	I	S	E		
S	E	P	I	A		D	E	R	M	A		S	D	S
		F	R	E	E		T	A	N		T	E	A	
T	A	F	T		L	A	P		T	H	O	N	G	
O	B	O	E		K	N	E	A	D		O	R	S	O
R	H	O	D	A		A	D	O		R	Y	E	S	
S	O	D		P	I	G		A	M	M	O			
O	R	C		A	L	A	R	M		A	S	S	E	T
		H	E	C	K	L	E	&	J	E	C	K	L	E
L	O	A	T	H		E	L	E	A		O	I	L	S
U	N	I	T	E		N	A	V	Y		P	E	E	L
G	E	N	U	S		A	X	E	S		E	D	N	A

3

S	T	O	M	P		L	I	M	P		S	A	N	S
P	A	L	E	O		U	V	E	A		U	H	O	H
O	C	E	A	N		L	A	M	S		R	O	P	E
I	K	I	D	Y	O	U	N	O	T		E	Y	E	D
L	Y	C	E	U	M		R	A	P	T				
		P	E	R	K	Y		A	H	O	L	D		
L	I	L	Y		R	A	N		F	R	I	D	A	Y
E	R	O	O		T	H	E	D	A		N	O	D	E
N	E	B	U	L	A		L	I	L		G	R	A	D
A	D	O	B	E		A	T	A	L	E				
		E	A	S	T		A	R	A	B	I	C		
F	A	S	T		A	B	S	O	L	U	T	E	L	Y
E	X	E	C		T	A	T	A		P	A	N	I	C
T	E	C	H		U	T	E	S		T	R	I	A	L
A	S	T	A		P	S	S	T		S	I	N	C	E

4

S	L	A	P		D	E	A	F		A	D	M	A	N
I	O	L	A		U	G	L	I		P	I	A	N	O
G	O	I	N	G	T	O	E	X	T	R	E	M	E	S
H	I	C	K	E	Y		E	W	E		A	W	E	
S	E	E	Y	A		G	A	R	I	S	H			
		R	E	M	U	S		S	E	E	D	Y		
O	H	M	E		M	A	C		S	K	I	D	O	O
G	O	I	N	G	I	N	T	O	H	I	D	I	N	G
R	A	N	O	U	T		I	D	A		I	T	S	A
E	X	I	L	E		L	O	D	G	E				
		A	S	I	A	N	S		S	W	A	T	H	
E	G	G		S	I	P		S	T	E	R	E	O	
G	O	N	E	W	I	T	H	T	H	E	W	I	N	D
A	B	A	S	H		O	B	I	E		O	S	S	A
D	I	T	T	O		P	O	N	D		N	E	E	D

5

L	I	S	P	S		S	P	E	C		D	I	V	A
E	C	L	A	T		T	I	L	E		O	B	I	S
S	O	U	P	A	N	D	S	A	N	D	W	I	C	H
E	N	G	A	G	E		A	T	T	E	N	D	E	E
		L	E	A	R		E	R	A	S				
C	B	S		S	T	E	M		I	N	T	A	K	E
O	U	T	S		E	E	O	C		N	A	M	E	D
M	E	A	T	A	N	D	P	O	T	A	T	O	E	S
E	N	D	E	R		S	E	C	S		E	R	L	E
T	O	T	E	M	S		D	O	E	S		Y	S	L
		L	A	L	A		A	T	U	B				
R	E	S	I	D	I	N	G		S	C	A	L	P	S
C	A	K	E	A	N	D	I	C	E	C	R	E	A	M
A	S	I	S		G	U	L	P		O	R	A	T	E
S	E	N	T		S	P	A	R		R	E	N	E	W

6

C	A	P	R	I		E	G	G		P	A	T	T	Y
U	N	I	O	N		S	I	R		O	M	A	H	A
S	T	E	M	S		A	L	I		L	A	X	E	R
P	E	R	P	E	T	U	A	L	M	O	T	I	O	N
		S	C	I		S	L	I	P					
I	S	H		T	A	X		E	X	O	T	I	C	A
N	C	A	A		R	I	G		N	O	N	O	S	
F	O	U	N	T	A	I	N	O	F	Y	O	U	T	H
R	U	N	T	O		U	N	E		K	I	T	E	
A	T	T	I	M	E	S		A	L	F		T	A	N
		O	P	I	E		O	U	R					
P	R	O	G	R	A	M	M	I	N	G	A	V	C	R
E	E	L	E	R		I	A	N		E	V	E	R	Y
A	M	I	N	O		L	I	T		E	E	R	I	E
S	I	N	E	W		E	L	O		S	L	O	B	S

7

```
P I T H ■ M O R A L ■ I P S O
S O H O ■ C R A T E ■ F U N K
S W I N G I N G O N A S T A R
T A S K S ■ A G L O W ■ O P A
■ ■ Y E A ■ M E L ■ E O N ■ ■
F E E D ■ B E D S ■ S T A R T
A L A ■ E E N Y ■ K O S H E R
G E R ■ N E T ■ D I M ■ A M I
I N S I S T ■ C O D E ■ P U P
N I K O N ■ C O B S ■ A P S E
■ ■ I N A ■ A M A ■ P L Y ■ ■
A S S ■ R E M I T ■ R E F E R
I T S A L L I N T H E G A M E
N O E L ■ A N G L E ■ A C M E
T A S S ■ N O S E S ■ R E A L
```

8

```
A H A B ■ L I M P ■ P L A N B
N O L A ■ A R I A ■ O A S E S
K N O B ■ P O N T ■ S C H W A
A G E O F A N X I E T Y ■ ■ ■
■ O R L Y ■ O N A ■ ■ ■ J O G
■ V E N O M ■ ■ ■ I G N O R E
M I A ■ M A U V E D E C A D E
A R T S ■ ■ G E T ■ ■ O N E S
G A S L I G H T E R A ■ N A E
I G U A N A ■ ■ ■ E Q U A L ■
C O P ■ ■ ■ T N T ■ S T U N ■
■ ■ ■ M E G E N E R A T I O N
K A Z A N ■ N O T A ■ O S L O
A D A M S ■ E P I C ■ L E G O
T E P E E ■ T E N T ■ D E A R
```

9

```
S U M ■ M O A T ■ ■ S T R A W
E R I ■ U N B A R ■ Q U I C K
D A M ■ S E A T O ■ U R G E S
U N O W H A T I M E A N ■ ■ ■
C U S H Y ■ ■ E B B ■ ■ I M A
E S A I ■ R E S O W ■ B R A G
■ ■ ■ P E E L E ■ H O R A C E
■ D O S O F M E D I C I N E ■
J E J U N E ■ D I T T O ■ ■ ■
R E A P ■ R H Y M E ■ C R I B
S R I ■ ■ T E A ■ ■ S H A N E
■ ■ ■ T R E S E L E M E N T S
A R M E Y ■ T R U C E ■ C U T
L I A R S ■ E R R O L ■ O N E
T A I N T ■ ■ S E N T ■ R E D
```

10

```
D E C A F ■ A D L I B ■ L U V
E L I S E ■ D I A N A ■ A S A
L O O S E L I P P E D ■ M E T
■ ■ ■ L A O S ■ ■ ■ L E E D S
F A S T E N S ■ ■ ■ C R U M B
E N T I R E ■ E L E C T R O N
L Y R E S ■ P L U N K ■ A C E
L O O S ■ F I L E D ■ M I T T
A N N ■ P I N E S ■ S E N A T
S E G M E N T S ■ S E R E N E
■ A T S E A ■ S E C E D E D ■
V E R S E ■ ■ ■ P A R T ■ ■ ■
C A M ■ T I G H T F I S T E D
R T E ■ A T R E E ■ O R O N O
S A D ■ S T O W S ■ N O N E T
```

11

```
S E R F S ■ L I R A ■ S C A M
T R A I T ■ O D O R ■ P O L E
R A C E R ■ T E A T ■ A L I T
A S K F O R H E R H A N D ■ ■
W E S ■ K E A ■ A R C ■ W P A
■ ■ ■ H E A R T T O H E A R T
A R T E ■ C I O ■ ■ E N T E R
R O W S ■ T O W I T ■ S E E A
M O O S E ■ ■ E N E ■ U R N S
O N B E N D E D K N E E ■ ■ ■
R E Y ■ D A Y ■ S T L ■ G A B
■ ■ F O O T E D T H E B I L L
C O O L ■ E L I A ■ C A L L A
T H U D ■ R E M I ■ T I D E S
S O R E ■ S T E N ■ S L A N T
```

12

```
S L A T ■ C R A M ■ D O O N E
H A I R ■ R I G A ■ U P T O N
U S D A ■ I T E R ■ R A T I O
T H E L A S T E M P E R O R ■
■ ■ ■ A L T E ■ O A S T ■ ■ ■
A R G ■ F O R E S T S ■ K I M
L E R O I ■ ■ A E C ■ N A N A
A L I F E F O R T H E C Z A R
R E S T ■ R U T ■ ■ L O O P Y
M E T ■ B E T H U N E ■ O T S
■ ■ ■ T E A R ■ R O N S ■ ■ ■
■ C H I C K E N A L A K I N G
P L I N K ■ A O N E ■ O N I N
C A D G E ■ C P U S ■ A T T A
S W E E T ■ H E S S ■ L O S T
```

13

```
G A S P . E L V I S . P E C K
I T T O . C O I N S . E V A N
J O I N T O W N E R . N E R O
O M E G A . M E D . S H R E W
E S S . L E A D I N T O . . .
. . . C O R N . B E E L I N E
O C T A N E . B L E N D S I N
T O R N . C R E E D . E I N E
T O O O F T E N . L O R N E S
O L D P R O S . H E S S . . .
. . . E A R L I E S T . A G E
S C A N T . A L A . E B B E D
P A C E . S T I R F R Y I N G
O V E R . T E A S E . E D I E
T E D S . A D D E R . S E E S
```

14

```
P L U M B . C L V . B L A H
R E S A Y . L A I . B O I S E
I M A D E H I M A N O F F E R
A M I . A M P . I N F E A R
M A R L O N B R A N D O . .
. . A R K . E T E . Y E S
A L E N E . D Y E R . C O R P
W E L C O M E . A S T O R I A
R A K E . A B A T . A M E N S
Y R S . B U D . A R E . .
. . T H E G O D F A T H E R
S P I R A L . R I A . O D E
H E C O U L D N T R E F U S E
A L E U T . J E T . P A N E S
W E S T . S R O . A D D L E
```

15

```
T I L E . B E L L . A N G R Y
A V E R . O D I E . M E L E E
M I N I . G N A W . I D E A L
P E A C E G A R D E N . E L L
A S S A I L . R O T C . .
. . G E R M A N . O L G A
R A J A H . E A S E . Q U I D
A P O R T . L I S . B U B B A
K A Y E . H A Z E . Y E S E S
E L B A . E X E T E R . .
. U S E R . L O C A L E
B I Z . L O V E H A N D L E S
O O Z E D . A R A T . R I M S
S T E V E . S I T E . O B O E
C A R E R . T E E D . M I N N
```

16

```
O L D S . C O L I C . T A C K
D A R T . A F A C T . E L H I
D R E S S B L U E S . R I A L
S K A . L I A R . S M E L T
. M O U N T A I N P I N K S
C H I N E S E . S E A N .
P O E T S . A I R R I F L E
A S S . A L L T O . L E N
S T T H O M A S . F R I T Z
. O M E N . A G R E E T O
C O L L A R D G R E E N S .
O S I E R . A C R E . A A A
S H O O . H A S H B R O W N S
M E N U . E L S I E . D A T E
O A S T . P A Y E R . E Y E S
```

17

```
S P I T . M A B E L . D I A L
T O D O . O P E R A . I D L E
D O O M . C H E A T . M E A T
. F L A S H I N T H E P A N .
. H E A D . E L L .
P L E A T . S U B . F E T C H
A I R W A Y . T A P . S O U
S N A K E I N T H E G R A S S
S E T . P E E . A L E R T S
E R O D E . O R B . A S S A Y
. E T S . A C R E .
. S T I C K I N T H E M U D
C H I C . A B A T E . B R I M
S I D E . T I M E S . L A V A
A V E R . E D E N S . E L A N
```

18

```
L A P P . W E D G E . A S A P
A L L Y . A X I A L . R A C E
H O U R G L A S S F I G U R E
R E S E A R C H . R Y D E R
. R U T . B A I L .
C A L A I S . F A L S E T T O
A W A C S . K A T E . R E P
W A T C H O N T H E R H I N E
E K E . L E E S . E A T O N
D E R A N G E D . A N G E R S
. F O A L . A N D .
M E N L O . A S T E R O I D
C L O C K W O R K O R A N G E
A L I I . A L I E N . S T O P
N E R O . R E A D Y . P O R T
```

19

IOWA · REST · LONE
MAIL · INTO · SAVED
ETRE · FROG · AMEND
THECOLOROFMONEY
HELM · IOU
SINBAD · ANARCHY
AROAR · OLLA · RIO
DOLLARDIPLOMACY
INT · ADES · PINKO
EYELIDS · STRESS
ORA · MALI
IFIWEREARICHMAN
RISEN · MRED · EASE
ADELE · MINE · ICER
NOEL · ANTS · READ

20

SPAM · NOTER · CHAD
LOBE · OCHRE · HALE
ACES · SHINE · ALAN
TOLOVEONESELFIS
NOR · SEAL
BOS · WILD · STEINS
OTTO · NOOK · INGOT
THEBEGINNINGOFA
HEROD · STEM · ERAT
ARNESS · SEPT · STS
REMS · LAM
LIFELONGROMANCE
ABLE · OARED · NEAR
DEED · CRONE · NERO
ETES · HEWED · ADDS

21

ABHOR · SEGA · SOLE
BLARE · CROW · INON
BELETTERPERFECT
RUSSIANS · ATTAR
EXT · USS · OLE
MAMAS · SPAS
OBIS · SCHELL · RAJ
PUSHTHEENVELOPE
STS · IODIDE · ODES
PEEK · QUEST
UNI · TDS · TAU
PINTO · HORIZONS
STAMPOFAPPROVAL
ERNE · WINS · ELEVE
TEEN · EGGY · DARED

22

ESTOPS · PROM · ODD
RAHRAH · OONA · VIA
SHORTENEDSTREET
ELM · CRIME · AORTA
PART · FDA
PARISIANPRONOUN
SLASH · AJAR · CHI
YODA · GASSY · SCUT
CHA · OLLA · COURT
HARMFULLIGHTRAY
AFT · BAAS
ASPIC · WHELP · SRO
GERMANAUTOMAKER
EVA · SONG · RAVINE
DEY · TREE · ENAMEL

23

SILAS · SAT · LUSH
ATALL · PSI · RENTE
CACTI · AHA · ENDER
SLEEPER · RELOOPS
RUY · DADA
ERA · PETE · SINNED
PACT · OILS · DEUCE
OVER · FLIPS · IDLE
DEREK · EVIE · LEAD
ELBERT · ETNA · STS
AVER · ANS
GATEMAN · STINKER
INAWE · ADO · MANGO
GONER · COD · AREAS
INKS · TWA · LEEDS

24

MARC · DOGMA · MALT
ARIA · ACRES · ALOE
WELL · MEANS · RAGE
ALIENABDUCTION
EVEN · MRI
VEINED · ORIENTAL
INST · STAND · AVA
CELEBRITYGOSSIP
ARA · OOZES · ASAP
ROMANCER · LEMONS
KKK · SAMS
ELVISSIGHTINGS
LOOM · TORAH · ELAL
BULB · ALONE · AUNT
ASTO · RAWER · DEED

25

```
C O P S E   S A G     S P A T S
A P R I L   H E E     T A G U P
G U A R D P O S T     E P O D E
E S T   E U R O     B E A R O N
      S T E P F O R W A R D
M I D S T S       R N A
I D E A   I S E E     G U I D E
C O M M U N I T Y C E N T E R
A L I E N   R O A R     I L K S
      E W E     O U T L E T
F O R W A R D P A S S
A P I A R Y   E L B A     I C E
R E S I N   B O D Y G U A R D
C R E T E   U N E     E G G E D
E A R E D   S Y R     S H O W Y
```

26

```
O W N E R   G L E E       B A D
T R A L A   R A F T     G O B I
H E S I N C O N F E R E N C E
O N T O   O V A L     E R N S T
      T I L E     U M P S
T E A   S A L I V A     H A G S
A T R I A     S I R     W H O A
S H E S W I T H A C L I E N T
K E N O     R H O     I N A N E
S L A P   K E T T L E     D A D
      R O S S     E I N E
S H O E R   T A T I     L E A S
H E S N O T A T H I S D E S K
E A S E   A N N E     P E R K Y
A D O   O D O R     A R O S E
```

27

```
S O C K   F I A T S     A P T S
A C H E   A N D R E     T R O T
T H I N K A G A I N     E E R O
Y E N T A   E Y E S H A D O W
R R S   P A S   S O U S A
    J U S T F O R G E T I T
D E P O T S   R U S E     I R A
E R L E   S E T     S N A G
M I A   J O I E   V S I G N S
I N Y O U R D R E A M S
    A N K L E   R N A   C U B
L I P R E A D E R   S H A N E
E S A U   N O T A C H A N C E
M E R S   D O N N E   R O U T
S E T H   O R A T E   P E T S
```

28

```
A L P S   A R A L   S A F E R
T O U T   F A R E   O C A L A
T A L E   C H E V Y C H A S E
A T L A S   N I E C E
C H U M P C H A N G E   A S U
H E P   A P O   G R E G O R
      A R O M A S   L E A N
C H I N E S E C H E C K E R S
A E O N   S T E R E O
M A N I A C   L E D   W B A
E T S   C H A R L I E C H A N
    S C O P E   D R A N G
C H O K E C H A I N   A L T O
D I D I N   I T S Y   Z E A L
S P E N T   D A M E   E R M A
```

29

```
R I B S   A V I A S   A M M O
O M O O   R I N G O   R A I N
Y O U R P L A C E O R M I N E
A N N E H E C H E   E E N
L I C   I S O   S L E D G E
S T E T   M A T T E   R U M
      R A E   P H E A S A N T
    W H A T S Y O U R S I G N
D I A M E T E R   N E T
A N Y   C E N T S   S H E A
R E F E R S   E P A   I T S
    E X O   A R E A C O D E S
H A V E W E M E T B E F O R E
E W E R   L E A H S   F U N T
P E R T   I N L E T   S T E S
```

30

```
S A G S   F A D S   D E C A Y
P U R E   A L I T   E C O L E
O R A N   R A N I   B O X I N
N O H A R M N O F O U L
G R A T I S   L U G   O D E
Y A M   S O L V E R   A V E R
    A Q U A E   A R E N A
  N O G U T S N O G L O R Y
G E N R E   A R L E N
A N Y A   A S L E E P   E B B
L E X   A S H   A P O L L O
  N O P A I N N O G A I N
U L C E R   G L E E   D I N G
M O N E T   G E A R   E N D O
P A N D A   Y A P S   N E S S
```

31

```
A B E T   B A A S   F A T A L
L O P E   A B L E   U T I L E
A L E X   B L I P   R O L L S
S T E A M B O A T W I L L I E
      S O L O     E E L
V C R   N E M E S I S   S A G
E R O D E     L A G   P A R R
G O O D T I M E C H A R L I E
A C M E   L E N   L E A S E
S K Y   S I N A T R A   D E N
      A T A   H E M S
S T A G E D O O R J O H N N Y
C A D R E   A B O O   R I C O
A R I E L   T O N I   E T A L
M O N E Y   S E E N   W E A K
```

32

```
S T I F F   G A G A   O N T O
C H O I R   A L E X   R A I L
A U N T I E M A M E   I N R E
M G S   E D E N S   T O N E S
    A N D     O I L Y
D A D D Y L O N G L E G S
O A S E S   A P O R T   O P S
A T T N   U N T I E   P A L O
F U R   U R G E S   G O T I N
  M O M M I E D E A R E S T
  L O P S     N O T
C L O D S   S E E T O   O D E
R A G E   U N C L E V A N Y A
O V E R   S A H L   E L M E R
W A R N   E G O S   D E E D S
```

33

```
S T O M P   B I O S   S H A H
P A C E R   R S V P   M A X I
E X T R E M E M E A S U R E S
D I S   S A W   R N A   E S S
    P E R U   H I G H
G U I L T Y P L E A S U R E S
O H N O     O R R   G A R P
L U C   M A N E D   Z O O
F R A S   A C E   H O S T
S U N K E N T R E A S U R E S
    A R T S   V I E D
A R F   M I A   E R A   A I R
S U R E A S S U R E C A N B E
O B E Y   S I L T   O W N E D
F E T E   A F T S   W E S T S
```

34

```
M O D E M   I R A Q   G E L T
E B O L I   S I T U   U V E A
D I G I N   A C T I   Y I P S
  F A S H I O N P L A T E S
C V I   T A D     S N A R E
R I G O R S   F O N D A
O C H R E   J A N E   S H A
S A T E L L I T E D I S H E S
S R S   I V E S   S U O M I
    C R E E D   L A B R E A
A P P L Y   C U B   T N N
F L Y I N G S A U C E R S
L U R E   R O C K   L I T U P
A M E N   A M M O   L O O S E
T E X T   B E E R   A S P E N
```

35

```
A R I D   P I T Y   P A A R
R E D U B   O R E O   A X L E
C O O K I E S A N D C R E A M
  S L E A Z E   S A R A
      N E U T   A D A G E
  B L A C K R A S P B E R R Y
B A L S A   M E T S   C O D
L I B S   J A P E S   E T U I
A L E   T A K E   P R I C E
H E A T H B A R C R U N C H
S E N O R   S P A R
    P O G S   S N E E Z E
P E P P E R M I N T S T I C K
O K I E   A U T O   T N O T E
W E E D   S T O W   A N O N
```

36

```
F L A P   S T A Y   S A L T S
L I M E   U R G E   E M A I L
A T O P   P O O L   N A S T Y
S H O P P I N G L I S Z T
K E N Y A N   R E E L I N
      G E W G A W S   A D A
  S H E A   I N R I   L U A U
H A Y D N P L A I N S I G H T
A L P S   A L T A   E C H O
I S E   S T A S S E N
G A R L I C   L A O T S E
  B A C H S C R A T C H E R
S T O R K   P L O P   C O M A
S O L V E   A I M S   U R I S
S M E A R   M O P E   R O S E
```

37

```
B L T S   L A M A R   R I O T
E I R E   A B O D E   A N N A
E M I T   M E A L S   W A L K
F I T T O B E T I E D   L Y E
S T E L L A     B E R R A
      E D S E L   N A T T E R
O A F S   T O A D   N E H R U
N I L   H E N P E C K   E L S
E D U C E   S I L O   F R E T
R E S E N T   N I N E R
    T O N E S   C L E A T S
S H E   A L L W O R K E D U P
L O R D   L A R G E   M A N E
O B E Y   E V E R T   A G E E
B O D E   R E N E E   N E R D
```

38

```
L A V A   B A S S   M A S K S
O B I T   A C H E   O N E A L
C O V E R G I R L   U N I T E
A D I E U   D I M E S   Z I P
L E D   S P R E A D S H E E T
      S T E A K   S E A
M A R T I N I S     L O I N
A Z T E C A N   S I L E N C E
C O E N   E A S E S O U T
    C H I   G L O A T
A F G H A N H O U N D   S G T
T O E   S C O T T   U S H E R
B R A S H   W R A P P A R T Y
A G R E E   L I R A   N E M O
T E S T S   S P Y S   G W E N
```

39

```
C A S H   C A S T   P S H A W
U L N A   O L I O   O C A L A
B O O M E R A N G   P R Y O R
S E W   T R I   A T T E S T S
    G H A N A   H O W
P A T R O L   S L A P D A S H
A L I A S   O P E N   R E N E
R I B S   D R I N K   I R O N
E V E S   H A R D   A V I O N
D E T H R O N E   S L E E P Y
    O I L   S T A I R
S T E P P E S   E B B   S K Y
C A R P E   H U R R I C A N E
A L I E N   A N N E   A R E A
B E E R S   M O S S   P I E R
```

40

```
M O O L A   S P E C   P I P S
A D H O C   T A P A   O S H A
T O N Y C U R T I S   N A I F
S R O   U S A   S P A C K L E
    A R U N   T I S H
    O S C A R D E L A H O Y A
P R E T T Y   L E N   A N T
R A I S E   S I S   C O N D O
O T S   A C H   C A G N E Y
    E M M Y L O U H A R R I S
    I A G O   A R T E
B R A C K E T   V O S   J I B
R O C K   R I T A M O R E N O
E T R E   I N O N   F I E R Y
W H E Y   A G R A   F A Z E D
```

41

```
A L E C   S W A M P   B A J A
D I A L   T I B I A   E V I L
A E R O   A L I S T   L E V I
M U L T I P L E C H O I C E
    H O L Y   E N E
B O V I N E   A C T O F G O D
A R E N A   I N A I R   A M A
S O N G   A B O R C   M E E K
I N A   S P O D E   H E L G A
C O L L A P S E   Q U A S A R
    A F R   C U L T
N O N E O F T H E A B O V E
G O A D   V I R U S   A L S O
A N K H   A R E N T   L I O N
S O S O   L E E K S   L O P S
```

42

```
A S S N   A D D U P   I S L E
T U N E   M O O L A   N L E R
B R O W N B E T T Y   S O A R
A L O H A   S E R E   T P K S
T Y P I N G   A E S O P
    R O U N D S   T R Y O N
S A V E   L O U   D E E J A Y
P I E   S L I M J I M   O R E
A D A P T S   B O X   B E S T
M E L E E   C O Y O T E
    O S T E R   N O R M A L
P O S T   A I R S   A R I S E
O N C E   S T E A K D I A N E
O M A R   T I B I A   E M E R
H E R S   S C A L Y   S I R S
```

43

```
A R T S   G R U B   A S T A B
L U A U   E A S E   N O O S E
P I C S   O N E A   A L F I E
O N T H E F I R S T C O U N T
      I N F     T A O
A L I   D R A M   G N E I S S
N A D A   E L I S   D A N C E
G U I L T Y A S C H A R G E D
E R O S E   S H O O   P O N G
L A M O N T   A W L S   T E E
      O R E     L I L
O R D E R I N T H E C O U R T
M A U D S   D O E R   C L E O
A R E N A   O G R E   K A N T
R E L A X   W A R D   E N T O
```

44

```
B E A M   M T G   R E D A T E
A B B A   I W O   E R I C H S
J A C K A R O O   M A D M E N
A N D O R R A   C A T S E Y E
        C O C K A T O O
M S G   A R T I S T   A L B
A C H E D   P E E K A B O O
C R A N I A   D I A L I N
K A N G A R O O   N A U R U
S P A   T A R I F F   E E S
      B U C K A R O O
T O T A L L Y   A R L B E R G
A F R I C A   K I C K A P O O
G L A Z E S   A L E   L I M A
S A Y E R S   L S D   I C E D
```

45

```
L A Z Y   M A R S H   F L O P
O L E O   A N I T A   L I V E
T I N K E R T O Y S   O M E N
S T O O L I E   T U T O R S
    O L E   A B Y S S
G I N A   S L Y   E A S E L
L E N O   T A I L O R M A D E
A N A   H O B B I T S   M I A
S O L D I E R A N T   C O C K
S A L E M   A B E   P H A T
    S O U S A   H U R
S H R I M P   A A M I L N E
H A I R   S P Y G L A S S E S
O N C E   E L I O T   T A S S
O D E S   T O N G S   O T T O
```

46

```
R O S S   H I R A M   A Q U A
A S H E   A L O N E   P U T S
P L U M I S L A N D   R E A P
T O N I C S   M E S S I A H S
    S E L A     A L S
S I L   M E M P H I S   I A N
A D O B E   P A I R   O N C E
L A V E N D E R S A C H E T S
T H E E   O R E S   A S S E T
S O P   S T E R E O S   S D S
    O R S   R U S E
E N T H R O N E   T I A R A S
V I I I   P U R P L E R A I N
I T O N   E L I T E   E Z R A
L E N O   C L E A T   D E E P
```

47

```
E M A I L   E D A M   S T L O
S A M O A   M I M I   T W I N
S P I N D O C T O R   R I F E
O S S   D I E S   A B U S E S
    P E L E   S C O T T
P O W E R S   T A L I S M A N
A S H E S   P I X E L   Y M A
C H I P   D A D O S   M A U D
E E R   D O Y E N   F A R S I
S A L T I N E S   C A L M E R
    P R A T E   D O V E
S P O I L S   D E M O   S A O
P R O P   T U R N A R O U N D
C E L L   O N U S   E L I T E
A P S E   P A G E   D E T E R
```

48

```
B A M B I   A N A I S   I T O
A R E A S   R E L E T   N I N
M A R K M C G W I R E   L A S
A B E E   O O H   F L A R E
    S U L T A N O F S W A T
A B O A R D   R I G I D
B O I L S   S T E R   C O D
U N L E A S H   C E N S U R E
T D S   P O S E   O T T E R
    S H A R I   B O R E O N
I T S O U T T A H E R E
V A M P S   M I A   A R I A
A L A   H O M E R U N K I N G
N O R   E R A S E   B E L I E
A N T   D A T E S   C R E T E
```

49

```
C A P R A   G L E N   P A P P
A L L O T   E A V E   A B I E
Y O U C A N T H A V E Y O U R
S U M O   O U R   A L M O S T
      C R O P   I D L E
A C H O O S   T R A I N M A N
C H A   D E T R E   E T U D E
A I R S   S A I N T   S T O P
S L E E K   S P E A R   E R A
T I M E O U T S   H A N D E L
      D A R E   L I M E
S H E I L A   B A T   P I S H
K A T E A N D E D I T H T O O
I R A S   U R A L   H E L L O
M E L T   S Y N E   O W L E T
```

50

```
L I N U S   S H A H   W A G E
A D O P T   A M M O   A V E R
F E E L I N G S U P E R I O R
F E L O N Y   L I L   A D E
      A T E A S E   P I N E D
G I L D S   K I T B A G
A D O   P I N   I S O L D E
T O U C H I N G S T O R I E S
O L D H A T   L O S   S A S
      A N S W E R   C H A R O
C E L T S   A T T I R E
O L E   E A R   S E N O R A
H A N D L I N G C H A R G E S
A T T U   N E E R   K I L N S
N E O N   T R O Y   S K E E T
```

51

```
E W E R   A S P S   G O M E R
F A D E   M O L T   I N T R A
T W E N T Y F O U R S E V E N
S A N T A   A W A I T S
      A R S   R O S I E S T
N E I L   H I N T S   D X I I
O R D   T A C O   D E T R E
O N E E I G H T H U N D R E D
S E A M S   E A S Y   A N Y
E S T E   B A D G E   E S S E
S T E R O I D   S O X
      G R A D E S   S P A R K
S E V E N S I X T Y S E V E N
I R A N I   N I L E   L O D E
P A N T S   G T O S   S N O W
```

52

```
  A L A E   I L S A   C A S H
G L E N N   D O W N   A R T E
M E A N T   E X I T   R E A L
S C H I R R A   S H E P A R D
      E E E   S H E R E
M A T   E T N A   M I N D E D
O S H A   A I L S   E T U D E
T H E M E R C U R Y S E V E N
H O T E L   E T T A   R E N T
S T A T I C   E A S E   T S E
      H O O K S   I D A
S L A Y T O N   G R I S S O M
H I P S   P A L E   S I T U P
E A S T   E V E N   O D O R S
A R E S   R E N E   N E W S
```

53

```
M O A T   F O B S   W H A L E
E L L A   O R E O   A E G I S
S E A M   R E A L   G L U E S
A G I A N T A M O N G M E N
      R O A D S   O L E
M E D A L S   P O E T I C S
E R E C T   R O A N   C U T
Y A N K E E I N G E N U I T Y
E T E   N I T E   O N E I L
R O B E R T S   S T E R E O
      U A R   A S K E D
  A N C I E N T M A R I N E R
D I A L S   O B I T   T U B A
E D D I E   S A L E   E D A M
B E A D S   E Y E S   D E N S
```

54

```
H E A P   P A P E R   S L E D
O L L A   I D A H O   M A D E
D A V Y   N O I S E   E M I R
S N A P   U R N   E L I T E
      H O P E L E S S T A S K
A C T O R   S E G O S
C R A N E S   S O P   S I L O
H O M E L E S S S H E L T E R
E W E S   L A D   S T E E V E
      E L M E R   C U R I O
E N D L E S S N I G H T
P E R I L   T A R   H O W E
E R A S   A G I L E   I N O N
E V I L   B A S T E   N E R D
S Y N E   S I T O N   G A M S
```

55

```
S T A I R   E C H O   S O F A
H A N O I   G O O P   E L L S
A P I N G   G R E E K W E E K
L E S   A G E E   R A N G E S
T R E A T E D   D E N
    T O T   L A T E P A S S
L O G O N   A I N T   E L M O
I T A L I A N S T A L L I O N
M O L L   B I T E   E L E G Y
P E A S A N T S   O W E
    L O A   U N I T I N G
E A S I E R   A N O N   N O R
S W I S S M I S S   S A N T A
T O L L   A C H E   K N E E S
A L O E   L E E R   Y A R D S
```

56

```
O H G O D   S I T S   H A L T
D E U C E   E D I T   A B I E
A W F U L   R O T E   M O N A
    F L I P F L O P S I D E S
    A L A S   S E L E N E
F A R R A R   S P U R T
E N A   H I P H O P B O O T S
A T M S   E A R   N O R A
T I P T O P S H E E T   Z E N
    O D E T S   R I B E Y E
M A G P I E   A G R A
C L I P C L O P B O A R D
C O V E   E L A N   D R I P S
O N E R   R I P E   E E R I E
Y E N S   S O A R   S L E P T
```

57

```
T A L L   A S P E N   A B L E
I D E A   S H A R I   A L E X
G O O D D A Y S U N S H I N E
E R N I E   O P E N   N O S
R E A D E R S   T R E A D
    A D U L T   S E T S T O
A D S   H E A P   Z I P U P
B E T T E R P L A C E T O B E
C L E A N   T E L L   T A R
D E V I L S   S L A P S
    E L I O T   S W A T T E D
O W N   S P A S   L O R N A
B E S T T H I N G F O R Y O U
I R O N   I N U S E   K I L N
T E N T   A T B A Y   S T A T
```

58

```
W A G E D   M O T O   G L U M
A L O N E   A S A P   L I N E
S L A V S   C L U E   O B I S
    L O C K H O R N S W I T H
P A P Y R I   U S E   D E E
A G O   Y O W L S   P L O D S
M E S S   S E A   S T Y
    S T O C K E X C H A N G E
    A H S   L O U   N U L L
K A F K A   L Y O N S   A L I
O D E   S A Y   T E H R A N
B A R R E L C H E S T E D
O G R E   P E A R   T W I L L
L I E N   H U L A   L E A V E
D O T E   A M E S   E R N I E
```

59

```
P A R T S   R A T A   S M O G
A T A R I   E D A M   T A B U
S E C O N D M O R T G A G E S
S A I D   E A R S   R I N D
E S S   A N N E   H E R E I N
R E T R E A D   D I S   S E A
    A R T   C U D   I N T
T H E F O U R T H E S T A T E
H E Y   R E S   A A A
O R E   W E D   A W K W A R D
R E P A I D   A L A I   P O I
    H I N T   O D A Y   L E S S
B E E T H O V E N S S I X T H
A R C O   D E L I   I S E R E
S E E N   E R A S   C A S A S
```

60

```
S R S   C Z A R   H I L T O N
T E C   R A T E   A M O E B A
I S H   A N T S   U B O A T S
G O O D B Y E C O L U M B U S
M U L E S   N U R S E   A S E
A R A B   I D E S   A G E R
S C R A M M E D   C P R
    E S C A P E   F R O M L A
    L P S   T O A P O I N T
P O M E   D E N Y   I T T O
U N E   F A U L T   A R I E L
L E A V I N G L A S V E G A S
S I D I N G   S I T E   A T T
A D O N I S   O N O R   N E O
R A W E S T   N E W T   T R Y
```

61

```
S T A T   P E R M A   A N O N
P A I R   A V O I R   L O B O
A X L E   M E A T C U T T E R
M I S S P E N D   T O A S T
      T A L E   T R U S T E E
M A I L C A R R I E R
E G R E T   A D E N   P P S
L E O S   R A V E D   C O O T
T E N   S O L E   G A M M A
      N A I L C L I P P E R
C O N C E R T   O A R S
A W A R E   S H U T T E R S
U N D E R L I N E R   O M I T
S E E S   I N U R E   N I L E
E R R S   B A B E L   E L E M
```

62

```
A L P S   P E T S   P A N E L
M O R T   I R A E   A D O R E
B O O R   N A U T   S E N S E
I T M A R K S T H E S P O T
  S O P H I E   D O T
  P I E   E R I N   W I G
S I T I N   I S O N   S H O W
U N K N O W N Q U A N T I T Y
M O O G   A G U E   O R G A N
O N S   T H E E   P R E
  S A O   R O M A N O
  S Y M B O L F O R A K I S S
S N A I L   E A S T   E C H O
M A P L E   A M I E   R H E A
U P S E T   P E E R   S E A R
```

63

```
B O L D   T S A R   K M A R T
O H I O   H E R A   H A N O I
S O M E   R U I N   A N O D E
C H A R L E S D I C K E N S
      O S S   A I D
A T T A C H   L A P S   D D E
P A R M A   S A A R   O R A L
T H E P L O T T H I C K E N S
L O S S   D U H S   I R A T E
Y E S   C E D E   E V A D E S
      B O O   C L I
  S P R I N G C H I C K E N S
L I E O N   A L E X   I D E A
A L A M O   P A R I   W A R S
S T R O P   E W E R   I M O K
```

64

```
  O D R A   S U S A N   B R A
  P I E S   C H O K E   R E N
W E A R Y W I L L I E   O P A
A R G A L I   A I M   R I L L
B A R N U M A N D B A I L E Y
E T A   M P S   S O R B E T S
  E M S   L I Z   C A D E T
      T H E F A T M A N
M A G E E   P G A   D O M
A D E L I N A   I L L   R O E
S A R A S O T A F L O R I D A
S P A R   R O B   E C H O E S
A T L   E M M E T T K E L L Y
G O D   M A I L S   I M E T
E R O   U N C L E   N E S S
```

65

```
P A I R   S L I D   A M A Z E
A L S O   T I M E   L A M E R
B A L L   E M I T   P R U N E
S M A L L P O T A T O E S
T O M E I   A I R   E M S
    L I T T L E W O M E N
S H A D   D O E   P I E T A
P I N E F O R   E D A S N E R
A T O N E   A L I   E T R E
T I N Y B U B B L E S
S T Y   P I A   S I M B A
  M I N I A T U R E G O L F
O P I N E   S I N O   A L I A
F A T S O   E N I D   V A S T
T R Y O N   S G T S   E R S E
```

66

```
W E E D   A M A S S   K A Y
A B L E R   R O B O T   I V E
N E W B O R N B A B Y   L E T
T R A I N E E S   M A O R I
S T Y   A N S   K E I T H
    B L E S S E D E V E N T
S H A R D   O N E S   R I O
P O L O   C A N O N   I T L L
A Y E   A U D I   F A Z E D
T A X D E D U C T I O N
  H O R S E   I S R   A S K
A L A M O   E L E G A N C E
G A L   B U N D L E O F J O Y
E V E   I M A G E   T O O N E
D A Y   C A G E D   R U E D
```

67

S	A	G	A		R	O	L	L	O		B	E	G	S
E	D	E	N		O	N	E	A	L		U	T	A	H
P	O	S	T	A	L	C	A	R	D		B	A	B	A
A	R	T	I	C	L	E		G	A	R	B	L	E	D
L	E	E	C	H			M	O	G	U	L			
			E	T	T	A		E	N	E	R	G	Y	
F	L	A	N		O	H	N	O		A	G	E	N	A
A	I	D	E		G	U	A	V	A		U	N	U	M
C	R	O	W	D		S	T	A	B		M	O	S	S
T	A	S	S	E	L		E	L	S	A				
		P	R	O	B	E			C	L	I	F	F	
P	A	L	A	N	C	E		C	O	R	O	N	E	R
A	T	O	P		A	R	C	A	D	E	G	A	M	E
S	O	L	E		T	R	O	V	E		O	N	M	E
O	M	A	R		E	A	G	E	R		N	E	E	D

68

C	H	I	C		G	L	E	A	M		Z	A	P	S
Z	O	R	A		R	A	N	D	I		A	D	U	E
A	M	I	N	O	A	C	I	D	S		G	A	Z	A
R	E	S	T	A	T	E	D		M	O	R	M	O	N
			I	S	I	S		H	A	N	E	S		
S	P	A	C	E	S		D	A	T	A	B	A	S	E
W	E	L	L	S		G	I	V	E	N		P	T	A
E	A	V	E		S	E	A	R	S		A	P	E	R
A	L	I		A	T	O	N	E		I	S	L	E	T
R	E	N	E	G	A	D	E		J	O	S	E	P	H
	A	L	E	N	E		B	E	N	E				
G	R	I	P	E	D		M	A	R	I	M	B	A	S
L	O	L	A		A	D	D	I	S	A	B	A	B	A
U	S	E	S		R	O	L	L	E		L	E	E	K
M	A	Y	O		D	A	I	S	Y		E	R	T	E

69

R	A	R	E		B	A	L	K		U	S	E	S	
O	R	A	L		O	B	I	E		A	N	K	L	E
B	E	G	I	N	N	I	N	G	O	F	T	I	M	E
S	A	S		I	N	R	E		R	A	I	N	S	
			A	I	D		D	A	R	E				
	B	A	D	G	E		E	E	N		D	R	A	T
S	E	P	I	A		O	M	E	G	A		E	W	E
C	E	N	T	R	A	L	A	M	E	R	I	C	A	N
A	B	E		A	D	D	I	S		A	D	O	R	N
T	E	A	S		V	A	L		T	B	O	N	E	
			I	L	E	S		T	A	I				
	S	W	E	A	R		G	A	G	A		V	I	A
S	T	O	R	Y	B	O	O	K	E	N	D	I	N	G
P	U	R	R	S		W	R	E	N		A	N	T	E
A	N	N	A		L	E	N	D		M	O	O	D	

70

A	M	M	O		A	B	E	T		S	C	A	R	
P	I	A	N	O		M	O	N	O		T	A	D	A
E	R	R	O	R		B	R	I	O		A	V	I	S
	G	R	I	L	L	E	D	S	H	R	I	M	P	
S	M	A		G	E	E		M	O	T	L	E	Y	
C	U	R	R	I	E	D	C	R	A	B				
O	R	I	O	N		H	A	L	O	G	E	N		
T	A	T	I		S	T	A	H	L		P	N	O	M
	L	A	S	S	O	E	S		M	A	G	O	O	
		C	L	A	M	S	C	A	S	I	N	O		
A	R	T	A	U	D		H	O	S		N	E	T	
L	O	B	S	T	E	R	B	I	S	Q	U	E		
E	G	O	S		R	A	I	N		U	S	E	R	S
R	U	N	E		E	V	E	N		E	N	R	O	L
T	E	E	S		D	E	N	Y		A	S	T	O	

71

I	D	L	E		J	U	M	P	S		U	L	A	N
S	E	A	L		O	N	E	A	T		N	I	L	E
A	B	S	O	L	U	T	E	L	Y		D	E	A	R
A	R	E		E	R	I	K		L	E	O	N	I	D
C	A	R	B	I	N	E		P	E	R	U			
			U	S	A		D	A	T	A	B	A	S	E
O	B	I	T		L	I	O	N		S	T	U	M	P
P	E	C	O	S		N	N	E		E	E	R	I	E
A	L	O	F	T		G	U	L	F		D	A	T	E
L	A	N	C	E	L	O	T		A	F	L			
		O	M	I	T		S	T	A	Y	P	U	T	
M	E	D	U	S	A		R	O	A	R		I	L	E
O	V	E	R		B	Y	A	L	L	M	E	A	N	S
P	I	N	S		L	O	C	A	L		A	N	A	T
E	L	S	E		E	M	E	R	Y		R	O	S	Y

72

M	A	M	E		D	E	G	A	S		O	W	L	S
A	L	E	X		A	B	A	S	E		O	R	E	O
C	A	S	T	I	R	O	N	S	T	O	M	A	C	H
S	W	A	R	M	I	N	G		S	A	P	P	H	O
		O	P	U	S		E	S	T	H				
G	R	A	V	E	S		B	A	A	S		S	H	A
E	A	T	E	N		T	O	R	I		S	P	A	N
S	W	O	R	D	S	W	A	L	L	O	W	I	N	G
T	E	N	T		C	I	T	Y		F	E	R	N	S
E	R	E		B	A	N	S		A	F	L	O	A	T
		W	A	V	E		W	R	I	T				
C	R	E	O	L	E		P	R	E	S	E	L	L	S
L	U	M	P	I	N	T	H	E	T	H	R	O	A	T
A	S	I	A		G	O	O	S	E		E	R	M	A
M	E	L	T		E	A	S	T	S		D	D	A	Y

73

E	N	T	E	R	■	P	O	P	E	■	M	A	M	E
L	O	R	R	E	■	A	C	E	S	■	I	M	A	M
B	E	I	N	G	■	W	H	A	T	A	D	U	M	P
A	L	S	O	R	A	N	S	■	E	L	I	C	I	T
■	■	■	■	E	S	E	■	L	E	O	■	K	E	Y
O	V	E	R	T	H	E	H	U	M	P	■	■	■	■
T	E	X	A	S	■	■	O	R	E	■	I	P	S	A
I	R	E	S	■	C	A	N	E	D	■	B	E	E	T
S	A	S	H	■	R	I	O	■	■	A	E	R	E	O
■	■	■	■	F	O	R	R	E	S	T	G	U	M	P
B	U	S	■	E	S	S	■	L	A	T	■	■	■	■
A	P	P	L	E	S	■	I	A	M	A	R	O	C	K
S	P	E	E	D	B	U	M	P	■	C	A	N	O	N
T	E	A	S	■	O	N	U	S	■	H	I	T	M	E
E	R	R	S	■	W	I	S	E	■	E	L	O	P	E

74

R	I	T	Z	■	S	T	O	P	■	A	O	R	T	A
I	D	E	A	■	L	I	V	E	■	P	R	I	O	R
F	L	A	G	P	O	L	E	S	■	T	I	N	G	E
F	E	M	■	A	G	E	N	T	S	■	E	G	O	S
■	■	■	E	P	A	■	■	S	T	I	N	G	■	■
T	U	P	P	E	N	C	E	■	A	C	T	U	A	L
O	N	A	I	R	■	O	L	D	I	E	■	A	D	O
W	I	G	■	C	A	L	L	I	N	S	■	R	A	P
E	T	E	■	L	I	T	E	R	■	H	E	D	G	E
D	E	T	A	I	L	■	S	T	R	E	S	S	E	D
■	■	U	P	P	E	R	■	■	A	E	S	■	■	■
C	A	R	R	■	D	E	C	E	N	T	■	H	O	T
R	U	N	O	N	■	H	A	I	L	S	T	O	N	E
A	R	E	N	A	■	A	R	N	O	■	A	L	E	X
M	A	R	S	H	■	B	L	E	W	■	B	E	S	T

75

I	N	G	E	■	A	M	I	S	H	■	S	O	N	G
C	E	L	A	■	C	A	N	T	O	■	H	A	I	L
B	R	A	V	E	H	E	A	R	T	■	O	K	L	A
M	O	D	E	L	T	■	N	A	B	■	V	E	E	R
■	■	■	S	K	U	A	■	D	E	F	E	N	S	E
G	A	R	D	E	N	S	P	A	D	E	■	■	■	■
E	V	E	R	■	G	E	E	■	S	E	W	N	O	N
L	E	D	O	N	■	C	A	W	■	S	H	A	V	E
T	R	O	P	I	C	■	R	A	F	■	I	T	E	R
■	■	■	■	N	E	I	L	D	I	A	M	O	N	D
W	E	S	T	E	R	N	■	I	N	I	S	■	■	■
H	A	L	E	■	E	U	R	■	A	R	I	O	S	O
A	S	I	S	■	B	R	I	D	G	E	C	L	U	B
L	E	N	T	■	R	E	P	E	L	■	A	G	E	E
E	L	K	S	■	A	D	E	L	E	■	L	A	Z	Y

The New York Times

Crossword Puzzles

The #1 Name in Crosswords

Millions of fans know that *New York Times* crosswords are the pinnacle of puzzledom. Challenge your brain with these quality titles from St. Martin's Griffin.

Available at your local bookstore or online at **nytimes.com/nystore**

Coming Soon

Tough Crosswords Vol. 11	0-312-31456-6	$10.95/$15.95 Can.
Daily Crosswords Vol. 64	0-312-31458-2	$9.95/$14.95 Can.
Large-Print Daily	0-312-31457-4	$10.95/$15.95 Can.
Monday through Friday Vol. 2	0-312-31459-0	$9.95/$14.95 Can.

Special Editions

Will Shortz's Favorite Crossword Puzzles	0-312-30613-X	$9.95/$14.95 Can.
Crossword All-Stars	0-312-31004-8	$9.95/$14.95 Can.
Bonus Crosswords	0-312-31003-X	$9.95/$14.95 Can.

Daily Crosswords

Monday through Friday	0-312-30058-1	$9.95/$14.95 Can.
Daily Crosswords Vol. 63	0-312-30947-3	$9.95/$14.95 Can.
Daily Crosswords Vol. 62	0-312-30512-5	$9.95/$14.95 Can.
Daily Crosswords Vol. 61	0-312-30057-3	$9.95/$14.95 Can.
Daily Crosswords Vol. 60	0-312-28977-2	$9.95/$14.95 Can.
Daily Crosswords Vol. 59	0-312-28413-6	$9.95/$14.95 Can.
Daily Crosswords Vol. 58	0-312-28171-4	$9.95/$14.95 Can.

Easy Crosswords

Easy Crosswords Vol. 4	0-312-30448-X	$9.95/$14.95 Can.
Easy Crosswords Vol. 3	0-312-28912-X	$9.95/$14.95 Can.
Easy Crosswords Vol. 2	0-312-28172-2	$9.95/$14.95 Can.

Tough Crosswords

Tough Crosswords Vol. 10	0-312-30060-3	$10.95/$15.95 Can.
Tough Crosswords Vol. 9	0-312-28173-0	$10.95/$15.95 Can.

Sunday Crosswords

Sunday Crosswords Vol. 28	0-312-30515-X	$9.95/$14.95 Can.
Sunday Crosswords Vol. 27	0-312-28414-4	$9.95/$14.95 Can.

Large-Print Crosswords

Large-Print Crossword Omnibus Vol. 4	0-312-30514-1	$12.95/$18.95 Can.
Large-Print Crossword Omnibus Vol. 3	0-312-28841-1	$12.95/$18.95 Can.

Omnibus

Easy Omnibus Vol. 1	0-312-30513-3	$11.95/$17.95 Can.
Daily Omnibus Vol. 12	0-312-30511-7	$11.95/$17.95 Can.
Daily Omnibus Vol. 11	0-312-28412-8	$11.95/$17.95 Can.
Sunday Omnibus Vol. 7	0-312-30950-3	$12.95/$18.95 Can.
Sunday Omnibus Vol. 6	0-312-28913-8	$11.95/$17.95 Can.

Variety Puzzles

Acrostic Crosswords Vol. 9	0-312-30949-X	$9.95/$14.95 Can.
Acrostic Crosswords Vol. 8	0-312-28410-1	$9.95/$14.95 Can.
Sunday Variety Puzzles	0-312-30059-X	$9.95/$14.95 Can.

Portable Size Format

Crosswords for the Work Week	0-312-30952-X	$6.95/$9.95 Can.
Super Saturday Crosswords	0-312-30604-0	$6.95/$9.95 Can.
Crosswords for the Holidays	0-312-30603-2	$6.95/$9.95 Can.
Sun, Sand, and Crosswords	0-312-30076-X	$6.95/$9.95 Can.
Weekend Challenge	0-312-30079-4	$6.95/$9.95 Can.
Crosswords for Your Coffee Break	0-312-28830-1	$6.95/$9.95 Can.

For Young Solvers

New York Times on the Web Crosswords for Teens	0-312-28911-1	$6.95/$9.95 Can.
Outrageous Crossword Puzzles and Word Games for Kids	0-312-28915-4	$6.95/$9.95 Can.
More Outrageous Crossword Puzzles	0-312-30062-X	$6.95/$9.95 Can.